In the Footsteps of
WILLIAM
WALLACE

The National Wallace
Monument at Abbey
Craig. *Inset*: Bronze
statue of William
Wallace fixed to the
Abbey Craig Monument.

In the Footsteps of
WILLIAM WALLACE

ALAN YOUNG & MICHAEL J. STEAD

SUTTON PUBLISHING

First published in 2002 by
Sutton Publishing Limited · Phoenix Mill
Thrupp · Stroud · Gloucestershire · GL5 2BU

British Library Cataloguing in Publication Data
A catalogue record for this book is available from the British Library.

ISBN 0-7509-2591-4

Front endpaper: The Upper Tweed valley and Selkirk Forest.
Back endpaper: Caerlaverock Castle.

Typeset in 11/14.5 pt Bembo.
Typesetting and origination by
Sutton Publishing Limited.
Printed and bound in England by
J.H. Haynes & Co. Ltd, Sparkford.

CONTENTS

One of the four illustrated plaques found on the Elderslie Wallace Monument. Wallace is seen here leading the Scots at the Battle of Stirling Bridge. The plaques were added to the monument in 1970.

PREFACE

The legends and traditions surrounding William Wallace share common characteristics with those other great legendary figures King Arthur and Robin Hood. All are seen as great leaders fighting for a just cause and their names have become synonymous with heroic resistance to oppression. All three have more legend than history attached to them, and it is these legends that have received great attention and much embellishment through the most powerful modern medium, cinema. The traditions and myths surrounding Arthur and Robin Hood have developed without paying much attention to the historical evidence. William Wallace, on the other hand, can be pinned down historically to the years 1297–1305. Yet, despite this fact, there has been such a tremendous development of legends surrounding William Wallace from the fourteenth century onwards that the historical figure has been almost completely submerged. The layers of this development have recently been fully traced in Graeme Morton's *William Wallace: Man and Myth* (Stroud, Sutton Publishing, 2001).

The popularity of Blind Harry's biography *The Wallace* (*c.* 1475) and Mel Gibson's film *Braveheart* (1995) has meant that the legendary William Wallace has been fixed ever more firmly in popular consciousness than the historical character and his deeds. Historians must recognise the importance of the development of traditions in their historical contexts as well as continuing to investigate the roots of these traditions. The search for the 'real' Arthur and Robin Hood by historians and archaeologists has shed little light on the 'heroes' themselves, yet it has revealed a great deal about the world in which Arthur and Robin Hood existed and their legends developed.

Through *In the Footsteps of William Wallace* Wallace will be examined against the background of recent historical research on both the Scottish political community in the late thirteenth and fourteenth centuries and the nature of Edward I's 'direct rule' over Scotland after 1296. In this context particular questions will be investigated. Was Wallace a loner or merely an agent for his overlords? What was his relationship with the political leaders of late thirteenth-century Scotland – Balliol, Stewart, Comyn and Bruce? Why did he provoke such hostility from Edward I? In addition, is there any historical accuracy in some of those firmly held traditions about William Wallace? History and tradition are equally fascinating elements of the story of William Wallace and here the text and photography reflect both.

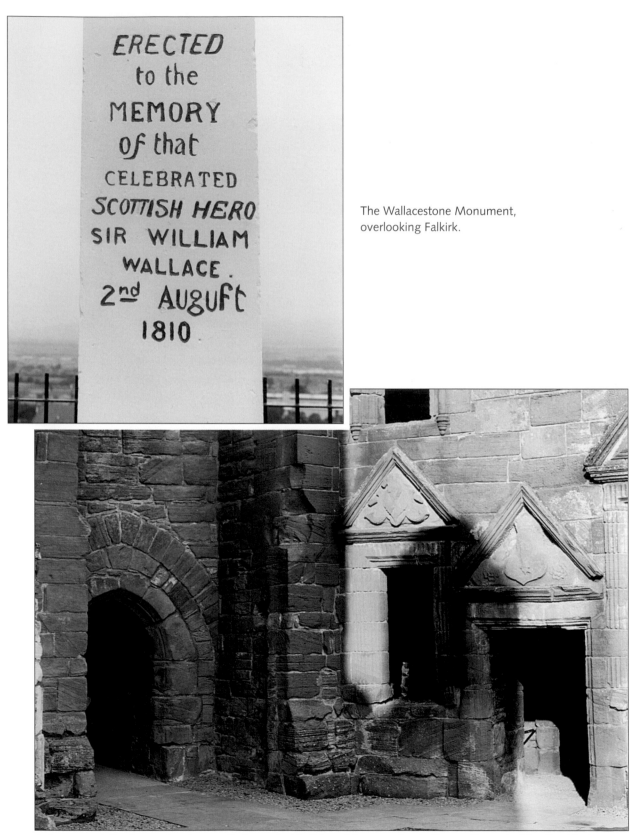

ERECTED
to the
MEMORY
of that
CELEBRATED
SCOTTISH HERO
SIR WILLIAM
WALLACE.
2nd Auguft
1810

The Wallacestone Monument, overlooking Falkirk.

A doorway at Caerlaverock, a key castle to control in Edward I's campaign in the south-west of Scotland between 1300 and 1304.

ACKNOWLEDGEMENTS

A number of individuals and institutions have contributed to the completion of this work. In particular, Professor G.W.S. Barrow's advice on this topic has been greatly appreciated and we are particularly grateful for his helpful comments on the book's final draft. This has helped us to prevent a number of errors and infelicities creeping into the text. The mistakes that remain are entirely our own, as are the opinions contained in the book.

We would like to thank, most heartily, Mrs G.C. Roads, Lyon Clerk and Keeper of the Records at the Court of the Lord Lyon, for her valuable assistance with research on seals. Staff of Historic Scotland were most helpful in sourcing photographs, as were the staff at the Scottish National Portrait Gallery, Paisley Museum and Art Galleries and the British Library.

We are again most grateful to Joanne Ripley for the speedy and efficient manner in which the final draft was put on disk. Thanks are also due to Jaqueline Mitchell and Alison Flowers at Sutton Publishing for their support for this project, patience and help in seeing it to completion.

Alan Young
Michael J. Stead

Dunfermline Abbey has traditional associations with William Wallace's mother. Blind Harry tells a story of Wallace's mother fleeing to Dunfermline disguised as a pilgrim.

1

WILLIAM WALLACE – THE MAKING OF A LEGEND

Anyone attempting to understand the William Wallace phenomenon in Scottish history must, first of all, establish how Wallace was viewed by his contemporaries. Only then can it be seen exactly when, how and why the legend and traditions now surrounding this character have evolved and developed over the last 700 years. As part of this process of unfolding layers of history and tradition that most significant source on the life of William Wallace the epic poem *The Wallace*, written in the 1470s by Henry the Minstrel (better known as Blind Harry), will be closely examined. *The Wallace* will be set in both the political and cultural context of the day, noting too the sources that had an effect on Blind Harry's work. In turn it will be seen what impact this late fifteenth-century poem has had on the late twentieth-century film *Braveheart* (1995) in terms of its portrayal of William Wallace. A number of questions arise. Why has Blind Harry's view of Wallace remained such a powerful, indeed dominant, influence on the popular perceptions of William Wallace? What other interpretations are there and why have these remained in the background? How far does this accepted view of William Wallace distort what is known of the historical Wallace?

Contemporary evidence for the historical William Wallace is restricted narrowly to the years between his sudden emergence onto the military scene in 1297 and his death in 1305. Within this time information is unevenly spread. Most material relates to the period from the summer of 1297, just before his triumph over the English army at the Battle of Stirling Bridge (11 September 1297), until shortly after his defeat at the Battle of Falkirk (22 July 1298). It is to these years that the only four historical documents emanating from William Wallace himself belong. After defeat at Falkirk, Wallace left Scotland, acting as a roving ambassador for the Scottish cause, principally at the French and papal courts between 1298 and 1302. Little is known in detail of his activities during these years. Following his return to Scotland in late 1302 or early 1303, Wallace

The Braveheart Statue. This representation of Mel Gibson as William Wallace was placed in the car park of the National Wallace Monument in 1998. It is the work of Tom Church and is a reminder of how significant Mel Gibson's film *Braveheart* has been in the development of the Wallace legend.

can be traced only through fragmentary references to his appearance in skirmishes with the English and in reports of Edward I's efforts to capture him. This pursuit ended with Wallace's capture by John of Menteith in 1305, after which Wallace was taken south to London where he was tried and executed. Reports of Wallace's trial and savage death form the bulk of the surviving contemporary comments on him.

One very interesting aspect of contemporary evidence on William Wallace is how little emanates from Scottish sources. The main Scottish strand in the standard narrative of Scottish medieval history was John of Fordun, whose *Chronicle of the Scots Nation* was compiled in the 1380s. Though written long after Wallace's death, Fordun's *Chronicle* is now acknowledged as an invaluable source of information for the period of William Wallace's influence. He had access to original thirteenth-century material and therefore must be recognised as the closest Scottish source to Wallace himself. Yet, though Fordun's reporting of facts may be accurate, his interpretation of events was naturally affected by the politics of his time. After Robert Bruce's (King Robert I's) death in 1329, Scotland had endured some years of great political instability – there had been a minority period, civil war and the constant threat of English invasion to support Edward Balliol's attempt to gain the Scottish throne. All of these threats to the Scottish situation seemed to be replicating the events that followed the death of Alexander III in 1286 which led to Edward I's interference in Scottish affairs. To make matters worse, the Scottish King David II had been captured by the English at Neville's Cross (near Durham) in 1346 and was subsequently held in lengthy captivity. As a result of these circumstances, Fordun's narrative strongly emphasises three themes – the growth of the Scottish nation and patriotism, the cause of Scottish independence and the importance of the Scottish monarchy in supporting these objectives. In view of the latter point, it is hardly surprising that Fordun's chief hero was Robert Bruce, who restored an independent Scottish monarchy in 1306, rather than William Wallace.

When Fordun's text is examined for information on William Wallace, he gives only a framework for his activities, an outline of his actions with little material about his background and, interestingly, in respect to later

The Kinghorn Monument. This monument to King Alexander III, who died mysteriously on 18 March 1286 while travelling in a storm from Edinburgh to Kinghorn in Fife, is a reminder of the political uncertainty in Scotland during William Wallace's early years.

The Abbey Craig Monument, close to the scene of his great triumph at Stirling Bridge, features this bronze statue of Wallace in chain mail holding aloft a huge sword.

writings, nothing on his appearance. Undoubtedly, William Wallace was a hero, as can be seen in the following extract:

> From that time there flocked to him all who were in bitterness of spirit and were weighed down beneath the burden of bondage under the unbearable domination of English despotism, and he [Wallace] became their leader. He was wondrously brave and bold, of goodly mien and boundless liberality . . .

However, to Fordun Robert Bruce was *the* hero of his *Chronicle*. Significantly, Fordun makes no connection between Wallace and Bruce in his narrative – they acted quite separately.

Though there are the beginnings of hero-worship contained within Fordun's descriptions of Wallace's actions, these can hardly be considered the foundations of a legend. Ironically, it is to contemporary English sources that the historian must go to gain not only more details of Wallace's activities but also to trace the origins of the legend. Foremost among these English sources are two northern chronicles, the *Guisborough Chronicle* (North Yorkshire) and the *Lanercost Chronicle* (Cumbria), while the annals of Peter Langtoft, which derive from Bridlington, are also of use. All English material is biased against William Wallace, targeting him as a hate figure. This surely reflects Edward I's attitude to Wallace at the time – to the English King Wallace came to symbolise, in 1297 and 1298, the spirit of the Scottish opposition and this became even more apparent between 1303 and 1305 when most Scottish resistance was crumbling away. It is interesting, if hardly surprising, that the most extreme English anti-Wallace sentiments were expressed by chroniclers living much further south, such as William Rishanger (St Albans Abbey in Hertfordshire), Nicholas Trivet (Oxfordshire), Matthew of Westminster and the Norwich monk Bartholomew Cotton. The anonymous author of the poem *Song on the Scottish Wars* shared their opinions too. Whatever the degree of hostility shown towards Wallace by contemporary English sources, there was a common desire generally to discredit Wallace's reputation both during his life and after his execution. To the Guisborough chronicler, Wallace was 'a common thief . . . a vagrant fugitive'. To the Lanercost chronicler he was 'a bloody man . . . who had formerly been a chief of brigands'. Within the *Lanercost Chronicle* was published a song describing Wallace:

> Thou pillager of many a holy shrine
> Butcher of thousands, threefold death be thine

Similar views, if more extreme, were voiced by Matthew of Westminster, who referred to Wallace as:

> . . . a man void of pity, a robber given to sacrilege, arson and homicide, more hardened in cruelty than Herod, more raging in madness than Nero . . .

The anonymous author of the political song *On the Execution of Sir Simon Fraser* pointed to Edward I's motives in using Wallace's death as a lesson to the Scots:

> Sir Edward our king, who is full of piety
> sent the Wallace's quarters to his own country
> to hang in four parts (of the country) to be their mirror
> thereupon to think, in order that many might see and dread

The targeting of Wallace as a hate figure and the triumphalism of England's popular songwriters at his death probably had the opposite effect to that intended. Instead of destroying Wallace's reputation, it heightened it, made Wallace a martyr for the Scottish cause and helped to create the legend of his life and deeds.

In Scotland it was not until the fifteenth century that the successors and amplifiers of John of Fordun began to promote a more detailed picture of William Wallace as patriot hero. The Scottish enhancers of Wallace's reputation were, principally, Andrew Wyntoun – *Oryginale Cronykil of Scotland* (*c.* 1420), Walter Bower – *Scotichronicon* (*c.* 1440) and most famously Henry the Minstrel (Blind Harry) – the vernacular poem *The Wallace* (1470s). It is clear that well before *The Wallace* was written there were tales, or 'gestis', circulating about William Wallace. Andrew Wyntoun comments:

> Of his good deeds and his manliness
> Great Gestis, I heard say, are made . . .
> Whoever his deeds would all endite
> Would need a mighty book to write

Edward I's Seal, the Great Seal for the Government of Scotland. Obverse: King Edward seated on a throne similar to that on the Second Great Seal of Alexander III of Scotland. He has curling hair, a large crown ornamented with three fleurs-de-lis, sceptre in right hand, the left on his breast, holding on by the cord of his mantle; his feet rest on the backs of two small leopards facing each other and lying on the footboard. (By permission of the Court of the Lord Lyon.)

Unfortunately, no traces of these 'gestis' have been discovered.

In the hands of Scottish chroniclers of the fifteenth century, William Wallace became a strongly Christian figure. Walter Bower, Abbot of Inchcolm, describes Wallace:

> Moreover the Most High had distinguished him and his changing features with a certain good humour, had so blessed his words and deeds with a certain heavenly gift . . . a most skilful counsellor, very patient when suffering, a distinguished speaker who above all hunted down falsehood and deceit and detested treachery; for this reason the Lord was with him and with His help he was a man successful in everything . . . with veneration for the church and respect for the clergy, he helped the poor and widows, and worked for the restoration of wards and orphans bringing relief to the oppressed. He lay in wait for thieves and robbers, inflicting rigorous justice on them without any reward. Because God was greatly pleased with works of justice of this kind, He in consequence guided all his activities.

This clearly demonstrates that Wallace was well on the way to unofficial canonisation before Blind Harry's biography in the 1470s. It is rather ironic to compare contemporary English descriptions of Wallace as 'a common thief' and 'pillager of many a holy shrine' with the depiction of him as an exalted Christian hero in the fifteenth-century Scottish chronicles.

Walter Bower not only portrays Wallace as a paragon, he also provides the first detailed physical impression of Wallace. This too is a prestigious, classical portrait:

> He was a tall man with the body of a giant, cheerful in appearance with agreeable features, broad-shouldered and big-boned with belly in proportion and lengthy flanks, pleasing in appearance but with a wild look, broad in the hips, with strong arms and legs, a most spirited fighting-man, with all his limbs very strong and firm.

This description seems to be modelled on the well-known vignette of Charlemagne given by his biographer Einhard, who in turn was influenced by the Roman writer Suetonius.

It is to Walter Bower we must turn for the popular tradition whereby William Wallace

Opposite: Dunfermline Abbey, famous as the burial place of Robert Bruce and other Scottish kings, contains this very fine stained-glass window showing Wallace, bearing a sword and guarding Scotia (represented by a young woman), with Bruce, St Margaret and Malcolm Canmore.

Another of the plaques mounted on the Elderslie Wallace Monument. Wallace is seen here raising the Scottish standard.

inspired Robert Bruce to take up the cause of Scottish independence in the aftermath of the English victory over Wallace's forces at the Battle of Falkirk (22 July 1298). According to Bower, Robert Bruce was on the English side at the battle – a debatable issue – and, pursuing the defeated Scots, encountered William Wallace who accused him thus:

> Robert, Robert, it is your inactivity and womanish cowardice that spur me to set authority free in your native land . . .

Bower relates that this stirred a profound reaction in Robert Bruce:

> On account of all this Robert himself was like one awakening from a deep sleep; the power of Wallace's words so entered his heart that he no longer had any thought of favouring the views of the English. Hence, as he became every day braver than he had been, he kept all these words uttered by his faithful friend, considering them in his heart.

It is important to note that no fourteenth-century source hints that Wallace had a role in rousing Robert Bruce's dormant nationalism. John of Fordun, the most well-regarded Scottish commentator on the period during which Wallace is said to have exerted influence, does not mention the episode. Another piece written at about the same time as Fordun's *Chronicle* was the epic poem *The Bruce* (1375), by John Barbour, the Archdeacon of Aberdeen. This comprehensive work praises in detail the life of Robert Bruce, but significantly William Wallace does not even warrant a mention.

Despite this, it is clear that the legend of William Wallace had already received some considerable development before Blind Harry's poem *The Wallace* took his reputation onto another plane of hero-worship. *The Wallace* was not only an epic in style but also in length, comprising almost 12,000 lines. It became, as will be seen, the most well-known representation of William Wallace. However, to appreciate fully the value of Blind Harry's work it should be placed in a number of settings – the Scottish historical context of Fordun, Wyntoun and Bower; the literary background of popular writing: outlaw ballads, the tales of Robin Hood, William Tell and Arthur and the writings of Chaucer; and the political circumstances of late fifteenth-century Scotland where the pro-English policies of James III of Scotland provoked hostile anti-English sentiments. According to M. McDiarmid, editor of a valuable critical edition of Blind Harry's *The Wallace* for the Scottish Text Society (1968–9): 'Harry's *Wallace* is firstly a poetical narrative and to be read as such, but an awareness of its propagandist bearing on the Scots' political situation of 1477–9 is essential to an understanding of the poet's free treatment of his subject-matter.' In the political sense, William Wallace was an ideal figurehead for the anti-English party. Indeed, in Blind Harry's hands, William Wallace even took on the appearance of Alexander Duke of Albany, the leader of the anti English party in Scotland during Blind Harry's time. Thus a new layer was added to the already exaggerated physical image of Wallace that had been fashioned by Walter Bower. Blind Harry used Bower's classical representation and contemporary knowledge of the Duke of Albany (later verified by sixteenth-century chronicle accounts) to compose a portrait that was influential for several centuries:

> In stature he was full nine quarters high,
> When measured, at least, without a lie.
> Betwixt his shoulders was three quarters broad,
> Such length and breadth would now-a-days seem odd . . .
> Great, but well-shaped limbs, voice strong and sture,
> Burning brown hair, his brows and eye-bries light;
> Quick piercing eyes, like to the diamonds bright.
> A well proportioned visage, long and sound;
> Nose square and neat, with ruddy lips and round.
> His breast was high, his neck was thick and strong;
> A swinging hand, with arms both large and long.
> Grave in his speech, his colour sanguine fine,
> A beauteous face wherein did honour shine.
> In time of peace mild as a lamb would be,
> When war approach'd, a Hector stout was he.

The value of *The Wallace* in understanding the historical William Wallace has been widely debated. In the eighteenth century, Sir David Dalrymple described Harry as 'an author who either knew not history or who meant to falsify it'. These two strands represent the extremes of the debate. John Mair, writing *The History of Great Britain* (1518), thought that Harry was blind from birth and that the information within *The Wallace* would have been obtained from popular oral tales rather than books. The work of M. McDiarmid (1968–9) has clearly demonstrated that Harry was not blind from birth and had, in fact, access to chroniclers such as Bower, Wyntoun, Barbour and Froissart. Indeed, Harry seems to follow and elaborate upon Bower at key points in his narrative, such as the emphasis on Wallace's personal qualities and physical characteristics, the episode after Falkirk in which Wallace awakens in Robert Bruce a latent sense of patriotism and duty, and the religious exaltation of Wallace. As far as the latter issue is concerned, Harry presents Wallace dramatically as the patriot leader appointed by God. Harry describes Wallace's vision in Monkton church in which St Andrew confers the sword of Scotland on him:

Into that slumber Wallace thought he saw,
A stalwart man, that towards him did draw;
Who hastily did catch him by the hand;
'I am', he said, 'sent to thee by command';
A sword he gave him of the finest steel,
'This sword', said he, 'son, may thou manage weel';
A topaz fine, the plummet, did he guess,
The hilt and all did glitter o'er like glass.
'Dear son', said he, 'we tarry here too long;
Shortly thou must revenge thy country's wrong.'

This cairn in Leglen Wood commemorates both William Wallace and Robert Burns, who was influenced by Blind Harry's writings. In *The Wallace* Blind Harry describes Wallace's attacks on the English garrison at Ayr from bases such as Leglen Wood.

The focus in both Bower's and Blind Harry's work is passionately anti-English. Bower's *Scotichronicon* ends with the words 'He is no Scot, O Christ, that finds this book displeasing.' As with the other themes, Blind Harry takes this a stage further, describing with relish a series of Wallace's violent anti-English acts of vengeance. Indeed, so overwhelming is this that Wallace's cause itself seems to become revenge against the English rather than defence of John Balliol's right to the Scottish throne, which is barely mentioned in *The Wallace*.

Historians have shown that Blind Harry's *The Wallace* is a complex blend of some fact with much fiction, distortions of other chroniclers and incorrect chronology. There are a number of major historical inaccuracies embedded in the poem, of which some of the most significant are: the Battle of Falkirk is dated five years (rather than one) after the Battle of Stirling Bridge and is turned into a Scottish victory; the Battle of Loudoun Hill is taken from Robert Bruce's career, as is the threat to the English war capital at York; Wallace is said to invade England as far as St Albans (there is no evidence that he came further south than the Tyne); the 'battles' of Biggar and Linlithgow are added to Wallace's war record; and he is given credit for coming to Scotland's rescue no less than three times. Yet, despite the misleading nature of the material in *The Wallace*, the general lack of detailed authentic information on many aspects of Wallace's career has led historians to hope that there might be some true facts hidden in the poem. The mystery surrounding Wallace's background and family origins is one area that has puzzled historians as they attempt to

The Barnweill Wallace Monument in Ayrshire, which was completed in about 1855. This memorial preserves another tradition, again graphically established by Blind Harry, that says Wallace made a revenge attack on a barn full of English soldiers. Apparently, Wallace, having set fire to the barn, shouted 'the barns of Ayr burn well', which gave the area its name.

understand the motivation for his dramatic emergence in 1297. Within the twelve books into which *The Wallace* is divided, the Battle of Stirling Bridge (1297) does not appear until the end of Book VII. Given that Blind Harry wrote the poem under the patronage of Sir William Wallace of Craigie, who was a descendant of William Wallace and probably familiar with Wallace family history and traditions, there may well be some accuracy in the details recorded in the first six books of *The Wallace*, which deal with William Wallace's youth.

Perhaps more important to the making and confirming of the legend from this period is the fact that Blind Harry's narrative was generally believed until at least the eighteenth century and that *The Wallace* was hugely 'popular'. Blind Harry wrote with the support and encouragement of Sir William Wallace of Craigie in order to prevent William Wallace's career and achievement as patriot hero from being completely overshadowed by that of Robert Bruce. As is well known, it is the winners (or their friends) who write the history of a nation. It is hardly surprising that Robert Bruce was *the* major hero promoted by Scottish nationalist writers in the fourteenth and fifteenth centuries – John of Fordun, Andrew Wyntoun, Walter Bower and especially John Barbour. Blind Harry and his patron sought to do for Wallace what Barbour had done for Robert Bruce a century earlier.

Blind Harry's main historical influences were the Scottish nationalist writings of the period 1370 to 1470, with Walter Bower being particularly important. However, other genres of literature also had an impact on the creation of *The Wallace* – the outlaw ballads especially, but also the work of Chaucer. As a result, Wallace came to be seen as a hero in the mould of popular figures of the time, such as Robin Hood, William Tell and Arthur. By the end of the fourteenth century, Robin Hood's reputation was already widespread and during the fifteenth century William Wallace came to be seen as a Scottish Robin Hood. Langland referred to the 'rymes' of Robin Hood in *Piers Plowman* in 1377 and it is important to note that two Scottish chroniclers known to have influenced Blind Harry, Andrew Wyntoun and Walter Bower, were among the first historians to mention Robin Hood and were clearly familiar with the ballads. Blind Harry's work follows the conventions of these ballads and it is hardly surprising that they share common features. Both present their respective heroes as proud outlaws, expert archers, using the inaccessibility of woods and forests to fight guerrilla-type warfare against their oppressors. The spirit of the Greenwood is strong in both. In both the protagonist employs a variety of disguises to avoid capture, displays generosity to the poor and fights for just causes. In *The Wallace* and the ballads of Robin Hood, the arch-enemy is a sheriff, chief representative of their oppressors.

It is interesting to note that, apart from the legend of Robin Hood, which had been in existence for over a century, the tale of William Tell was also being embellished at about the time Blind Harry was writing. In addition, rather more well-established stories were gaining new life in the late fifteenth century. In 1485 Malory's *Le Morte D'Arthur* was published in England, giving greater prominence to this long-lived saga. There are certainly parallels between the amount of violence in this work and Blind Harry's poem. *The Wallace* should be examined amid this array of legends and the image of William Wallace was undoubtedly affected by exposure to this literary genre. No doubt too this style was popular and perhaps enhanced with some stylistic elements from Chaucer.

The Wallace was one of the first printed books in Scotland in about 1508–9 and became one of the most successful books in that country. There were at least twenty-three editions of the poem before 1707 and, according to Dr James Moir who produced the first Scottish Text Society edition of the poem, only the Bible was found more often in Scottish homes. The popularity of Harry's *The Wallace* was no doubt increased with the translation by William Hamilton of Gilbertfield in 1722, *A New Edition of the Life and Heroick Actions of the Renoun'd Sir William Wallace, General and Governor of Scotland*. The many editions of this version ensured the ascendancy of *The Wallace* throughout the eighteenth and nineteenth centuries. It outstripped Barbour's *The Bruce* in popularity and this also extended beyond Scotland.

The story of William Wallace inspired Robert Southey in his *The Death of Wallace* (1798):

> He call'd to mind his deeds
> Done for his country in the embattled field,
> He thought of that good cause for which he died,
> And it was joy in death

William Wordsworth also made reference to Wallace in his *Prelude* (1805):

> How Wallace fought for Scotland, left the name
> Of Wallace to be found, like a wild flower,
> All over his dear country, left the deeds
> Of Wallace, like a family of Ghosts,
> To people the steep rocks and river banks,
> Her natural sanctuaries, with a local soul
> Of independence and stern liberty.

These words reflect the reality of Wallace's popular association with the Scottish landscape. The name of Wallace is linked with hundreds of placenames across Scotland (though the majority of them are to be found in central and south-west Scotland) including: Wallace's Tower, Wallace's Monument, Wallace's Hill, Wallace's Stone, Wallace's Trench, Wallace's Cave, Wallace Moor, Wallace Seat, Wallace's Well, Wallace Wood, Wallace Road, Wallace's Pass, Wallace's Leap, Wallace's Camp, Wallace's Rocks, Wallace's Brae and even Wallace's Bed and Wallace's Beef Barrell! These names bear remarkable witness to William Wallace's public appeal.

The popularity of William Wallace was also perpetuated through Robert Burns. Blind Harry's *The Wallace* was the most renowned work in Scotland before the era of Burns and Walter Scott. Robert Burns was, like many others, influenced by the life of William Wallace and ranked him alongside Hannibal as one of his chief heroes (as cited by Elspeth King in *Blind Harry's Wallace, William Hamilton of Gilbertfield* [Edinburgh, Luath Press, 1998]):

Selkirk plaque. Selkirk Forest, the ancient Ettrick Forest, was often used as a base by William Wallace during his campaigns against English forces in Scotland. Tradition has it that this was the site where Wallace was created Guardian of Scotland but it is not known precisely where or when he received this honour.

The face of the Dryburgh Statue. The image of Wallace depicted here, typical of many nineteenth-century portraits, tends to add both years and *gravitas* to him.

The story of Wallace poured a Scottish prejudice in my views which will boil along, there until the floodgates of life shut in eternal rest.

It might be thought that the formal political Treaty of Union between England and Scotland in 1707 would lead to the need for a different kind of symbolic national hero in Scotland. During the long periods of actual or threatened warfare between Scotland and England during the fourteenth, fifteenth and sixteenth centuries it was natural to promote figures who would be held up as fighting symbols of resistance. Blind Harry's portrait of Wallace at the end of the fifteenth century represented an extreme form of violently anti-English hero and divinely appointed martyr for his country's cause. However, the Treaty of Union did not bring to an end Scotland's need to defend and maintain a distinct identity. Marinell Ash noted in *The Strange Death of Scottish History* (Edinburgh, Ramsay Head Press, 1980) that the nineteenth century was a time 'that Scotland was ceasing to be distinctly and confidently herself . . . also the period when there grew an increasing emphasis on the emotional trappings of the Scottish past'.

One aspect of this was the raising of monuments to national heroes, and William Wallace was central to this movement. Wallace statues and memorials were set up as enthusiastically as Wallace placenames were adopted. A number of structures were erected in the early nineteenth century including the Wallace Monument at Wallacestone on 2 August 1810 and more notably the 21-ft memorial at Dryburgh on 22 September 1814. Even more magnificent was the National Wallace Monument which was built by public subscription on Abbey Craig at Stirling and promoted by the Revd Charles Rogers, founder of the Royal Historical Society. Constructed between 1861 and 1869 and eventually rising to a height of 220 ft, the National Wallace Monument attracted much public attention from the outset – a crowd of over 50,000 people attended a great ceremony to mark the laying of the foundation stone.

Many other monuments testify to the cult of William Wallace in the nineteenth century. The Wallace Tower in Ayr, for example, was renovated

The Dryburgh Statue, commissioned by the eleventh Earl of Buchan in 1814, was sculpted from red sandstone and is 21 ft high.

in Gothic style in 1834. Another Wallace statue in Stirling town centre depicts Wallace in Grecian fashion. The Wallace Memorial Window in Paisley Abbey, set up in 1873, portrays Wallace as Samson. Wallace was seen as a hero in classical and biblical style. It is apparent from the monuments and memorials of this time that Wallace was represented with a seniority of years and a certain 'gravitas', which was in keeping with the Victorian period.

William Wallace was still a cult figure in Scotland in the nineteenth century, but his image had changed to suit the time. Nationalism in nineteenth-century Scotland meant something quite different from what it had in Blind Harry's time and the symbol of William Wallace adapted too. The Scottish Patriotic Society through the Revd David MacRae played a key role in the funding of the monument to Wallace's capture at Robroyston, which was unveiled in 1900. The National Association for the Vindication of Scottish Rights supported the National Monument to Wallace but could also, without any sense of incongruity, voice admiration for Scotland's partner in the Union, England. Recent research has revealed that backing for the Union was the majority view in Scotland and that supporters of this were as fervent as any in promoting the cult of William Wallace.

This window at Paisley Abbey depicts Wallace as Samson and dates from 1873. The Cluniac abbey of Paisley was founded by Walter Fitz Alan, Steward of Scotland, in about 1163. The nearness of Elderslie and the Wallace link with the Stewarts has led to the tradition that William Wallace may have received early schooling here.

Standing at a height of 113 ft, the Wallace Tower in Ayr was built in Gothic style in the 1830s and contains a statue of Wallace high up on the front. This is one of two statues of Wallace in the town, the other one being placed in a niche in a building in Newmarket Street in 1819.

GULIELMUS VALLAS DE ELLERSLIE.

Nationalism and Unionism could go hand in hand. According to this view, a Union profitable to Scotland had been achieved partly as a result of Wallace's contribution to the resistance movement, which ultimately prevented the English conquest of Scotland. The names of prominent men who supported the Union and the building of Wallace memorials included the Earl of Elgin, who was to the fore when the movement to build the Wallace Monument started in 1856. His views expressed the opinion of many: '. . . that it is the successful struggle carried on under Bruce and Wallace, that it is that the Union between Scotland and England has not only been honourable to the former but profitable to the latter . . . that if the whole truth were to be told in this matter, we might show that England owes to Wallace and Bruce a debt of obligation only second to that which is due to them by Scotland'. (quoted by G. Morton, as cited in David McCrone, 'Scotland – the Brand', p. 45 in *Images of Scotland*, Journal of Scottish Education Occasional Paper No. 1). This notion of nationalism within the political framework of the United Kingdom remains a viewpoint supported by mainstream politics in the twentieth century. Both Bruce and Wallace are incorporated. In 1993, the Conservative ex-Secretary of State, Ian Lang, claimed that the Union of the nations of Scotland and England in 1707 was a legacy of Bannockburn. In 1997, the date 11 September

Left: This statue of William Wallace stands above the doorway of St Nicholas' Church in Lanark. It dates from about 1820.

Right: A nineteenth-century Johnston print of William Wallace (SP345). (Courtesy of the Scottish National Portrait Gallery.)

'Wallace Defending Scotland' (central panel) by David Scott (1806–49). This is another example of Wallace being portrayed in the classical style during the nineteenth century. (Reproduced by courtesy of Renfrew District Council Museums and Art Galleries Service.)

(undoubtedly chosen to stir memories of William Wallace and his victory on that date at Stirling Bridge) was deemed appropriate for the great majority of the Scottish people to vote for a Scottish parliament (which they did).

William Wallace has become a national symbol for Scotland and this has been acknowledged by political parties in general. From the nineteenth century to the present, Wallace has had widespread support across political parties and across class. To the working classes in nineteenth-century Scotland he came to represent the 'common man' fighting for freedom against oppression, while to the middle classes he came to personify a 'middle-class' hero who had saved the country from the folly of the aristocratic governing class. The legend and image of William Wallace have evolved from the fifteenth century and are still developing. In this context the film *Braveheart* (1995) represents not so much a twentieth-century expansion of the legend, a 'Hollywood history' version of William Wallace's life, but a reversion to Blind Harry's character, a late fifteenth-century two-dimensional Wallace. Based on Randall Wallace's novel *Braveheart* (London, Signet, 1995), which in turn used Blind Harry's *The Wallace* as its main source, Mel Gibson's film *Braveheart* follows closely

Detail from the Elderslie Wallace Monument, completed in 1912. This memorial celebrates the traditional birthplace of William Wallace and has often been the focus of rallies held by the Scottish Nationalist Party.

Taking its name from the nearby abbey ruins at Cambuskenneth, the National Wallace Monument at Abbey Craig has become the focal point of both 'Wallace tourism' and Scottish nationalism since its opening in 1869.

the legend created by Blind Harry. Not all details are the same though there are some significant similarities – the bridge at Stirling that played such a major role in the Scottish victory at the Battle of Stirling Bridge did not feature in either Blind Harry's poem or the film *Braveheart*. In general, however, the film represents a rather less exaggerated portrait of its hero than Blind Harry does. In the poem Wallace's invasion of England reaches St Albans, whereas *Braveheart*'s Wallace only reaches York. Nevertheless, both accounts have strayed a long way from the footsteps of the real William Wallace.

The widespread success of Blind Harry's *The Wallace* from the 1470s and the popular acclaim of the film *Braveheart* from 1995 to the present have combined to produce a very powerful image of one basic interpretation of William Wallace. It is very difficult, therefore, to reach beyond this to understand the many and varied layers of the legend and the complexities of a multi-faceted hero. Only an integrated study of Wallace that incorporates the views of thirteenth-century English chroniclers, fourteenth- and fifteenth-century Scottish nationalist writers (where fact first starts to blend with legend), nineteenth-century nationalists and twentieth- and twenty-first-century commentators on William Wallace and his legend can hope to achieve a more complete picture of Wallace in history and legend.

2

PEASANT RASCAL OR NOBLE HERO?

L ittle is known about William Wallace's family background and life before his sudden and dramatic appearance on the military and political stage in the summer of 1297. Lack of detail in the respected account of John of Fordun has led to much speculation about Wallace's origins and, by implication, his motivation in 1297. According to Fordun:

> The same year [1297], William Wallace lifted up his head from his den – as it were – and slew the English sheriff of Lanark . . . in the town of Lanark.

The chronicler goes on to make a brief but interesting comment about Wallace's family:

> . . . and, though, among the earls and lords of the kingdom, he was looked upon as low-born, yet his fathers rejoiced in the honour of knighthood.

Fordun later implied that William Wallace was a younger son and that his father was dead by 1297:

> His elder brother, also, was girded with the knightly belt, and inherited a landed estate which was large enough for his station.

Andrew Wyntoun, writing in about 1420, also did little to conceal the relatively humble origins of William Wallace:

> For he wes cummyn of gentilmen
> In sympel state set he wes then.
> Hys fadyre wes a manly knycht;
> Hys modyre wes a lady brycht

Wallace's own status, as well as that of his family, was given a boost by Walter Bower, which is hardly surprising given Bower's role in the origins

The traditional birthplace of Wallace's father at Riccarton, Ayrshire, is marked by this plaque just outside the fire station. However, the name of Wallace's father is disputed.

and development of the Wallace legend. According to Bower, William Wallace was already a knight when he first burst onto the political scene by killing the English Sheriff of Lanark: he came from 'a distinguished family, with relatives who shone with knightly honour'. Bower also adds that William Wallace was 'the son of the noble knight [Malcolm Wallace]' and that he had an older brother called Andrew. The name 'Malcolm', however, was inserted after Bower's time and may have been confused with the name of an older brother who was recorded as being present at a baronial council in 1299. The author of the *Book of Pluscarden* thought that William Wallace's father was another William Wallace, while a later version of Bower recorded Andrew Wallace, Lord of Craigie (Ayrshire), as his father's name. Recent discussion has centred on the legend surrounding the seal William Wallace attached to his (and Andrew Moray's) letter to Lübeck and Hamburg (1297). The seal seems to read 'Willelmi le Walays filii Alani', i.e. William Wallace, son of Alan. The more contemporary English Lanercost chronicler records the fact that a brother of William Wallace, named John, met the same fate as his brother at the hands of the English. Confusion about the name of William Wallace's father highlights, perhaps, the fact that members of his family were not major landowners and not part of the aristocratic governing class of Scotland. It is probably for this reason that Bower elevates the Wallace family's status as far as he can but chooses rather to distract attention from its origins to describe, in great detail, William Wallace's personal and physical qualities.

Following on from Bower, Blind Harry further bolstered William Wallace's family origins:

> Sir William Wallace, much renown'd in war;
> Whose bold progenitors have long time stood,
> Of honourable and true Scottish blood
> And in first rank of ancient barons go
> Old knights of Craigy, baronets [bannerets] also . . .
> So much for the brave Wallace's father's side,
> Nor will I here his mother's kindred hide:
> She was a lady most complete and bright,

> The daughter of that honourable knight,
> Sir Ronald Crawford, high sheriff of Ayr,
> Who fondly doted on his charming fair,
> Soon wedded was the lovely blooming she,
> To Malcolm Wallace then of Ellerslie.

Thus in the development of John of Fordun's comments that William Wallace was 'looked upon as low-born' among the earls and lords of the kingdom, by the end of the fifteenth century William Wallace had been raised to an acceptably aristocratic status.

By contrast, contemporary English sources emphasise his non-nobility. A song cited in the *Lanercost Chronicle* triumphs in the English success against Wallace at the Battle of Falkirk (1298) and draws attention to Wallace's lowly origins: 'The Scottish nation, basely led, hath fallen in the dust'. Another song from the same source rejoices in Wallace's death in 1305 and contains a similar message: 'Scotland! be wise, and choose a nobler chief'.

As has already been mentioned, the most extreme anti-Wallace sentiments have tended to originate in southern England and this also applies to English comments about William Wallace's family background. According to the *Rishanger Chronicle* William Wallace was 'sprung from low-born stock . . . an expert archer who made his living by bow and quiver' (this view is corroborated by William Wallace's use of a bow symbol in his 1297 seal – see p. 31). This was hardly a noble pursuit, and an extract from the Royal Manuscript complements this view and describes Wallace as a 'peasant rascal from nowhere'. Both fifteenth-century Scottish nationalist writers and biased contemporary English chroniclers produce exaggerated propagandist stances. There is, however, some common ground between Fordun and the English chroniclers – the nearest to contemporary Scottish source (Fordun) and English concurrent writers agree that William Wallace did not belong to the aristocratic governing elites, which controlled political offices in both England and Scotland.

A great many details about the Wallaces are missing because of the limited land they held. Property transactions provide historians with valuable clues about family relationships and the extent of noble landowning. Therefore, the most obvious next step is to examine the family who were overlords to the Wallaces, the Stewarts. This clan became a major noble family in Scotland during the course of the twelfth and thirteenth centuries. Originally the Stewarts were a Breton family – Walter Fitz Alan, the first of the Stewarts of Scotland was the third son of Alan, son of Flaald, son of Alan, son of Flaald. They had been stewards of the lords of Dol in Brittany. The Fitz Alans were closely attached to the household of Henry, youngest son of William the Conqueror, who became King of England in 1100, reigning until 1135. The family benefited from Henry I's patronage, just as the Wallaces did from the

Overleaf, background image: Dumbarton Castle on the north shore of the Clyde.

THE STEWARTS

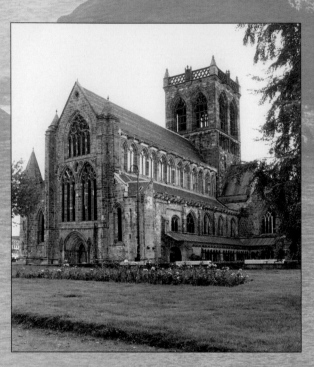

Paisley Abbey. It was only raised to the rank of an abbey in 1245, and its promotion mirrors the ascendancy of the Stewart family, the founders of the abbey in about 1163, during the thirteenth century. The abbey was burnt by the English in 1307.

The Stewart family, like the Comyns and Morays, benefited from Scottish royal patronage in the twelfth century. With their hereditary position as Steward of Scotland and large estates, especially in western Scotland (Renfrewshire, Lanarkshire and Ayrshire), derived from royal grants to Walter Fitz Alan, first 'Steward' of Scotland *c.* 1136–77, the Stewarts were a powerful group by 1200. The Scottish crown in the thirteenth century continued to be dependent on its magnates for wielding royal power and authority in the provinces – the Stewarts were at the forefront of the Scottish monarchy's attempt to extend, consolidate and define royal authority in the west of the country.

The Seal of Walter Stewart, c. 1170. Walter Fitz Alan, the first Steward of the Scottish royal household was the originator of the Stewart 'empire' between 1136 and 1177, establishing estates in Renfrewshire and Lanarkshire (Strathgryfe) and Ayrshire (Kyle Stewart). (By permission of the Court of the Lord Lyon.)

The Privy Seal of James Stewart, c. 1296. It shows a shield of arms: a fess chequy and a shield within a rounded and pointed trefoil panel. The legend reads: 'Secretum Jacobi Senescalli Scocie' (Seal of James Steward of Scotland). (By permission of the Court of the Lord Lyon.)

Alexander Stewart, the head of the main branch of the family, commanded the Scottish army against the Norwegian forces of Hakon IV at the Battle of Largs in 1263. Walter Stewart gained the earldom of Menteith in 1260–1 and by 1262 had extended his influence, through royal authority, into Knapdale and Arran, at the expense of the MacSweens. He probably also ousted the Bissets from Arran. The Stewarts controlled the sheriffdoms of Ayr and Dumbarton for much of the period from the 1260s to the 1280s. The Stewarts would be greatly disadvantaged if Scottish kingship lost independence and, therefore, its powers of patronage. The Stewarts were not ready, however, during William Wallace's lifetime, to back the dynastic ambitions of the Bruces to whom they were linked through locality (south-west Scotland) and marriage (by 1261). They did eventually (by 1307) support Robert Bruce's coup of 1306. Their alliance with the Bruces was further consolidated by the marriage, in 1315, of Marjorie, Robert Bruce's daughter, to Walter Stewart. The Stewart dynasty originated from this union in 1371.

Dundonald Castle. Little survives of this thirteenth-century castle of the Stewarts. The present remains, the tower house, date mainly from the fourteenth century. When Robert II (Stewart) became King in 1371 he had it rebuilt. Dundonald was probably the head of the Kyle Stewart group of estates in Ayrshire.

support of the Stewarts. The eldest member of the Fitz Alan family, Jordan, inherited the lands in Brittany, the second, William, gained much land in England, especially in Shropshire and Sussex. The third and youngest son, Walter, held the least land, some in Shropshire some near Arundel, but like many younger sons moved to seek his fortune elsewhere – in his case, Scotland.

David I, King of Scots (1124–53), had been a close friend of Henry I and between 1093 and 1107 he had spent much time at the courts of William Rufus and Henry I. The influence of the Anglo-Norman court and Anglo-Norman society, according to the rather prejudiced southern commentary of William of Malmesbury, 'rubbed off all the tarnish of Scottish barbarism'. David was, in fact, knighted by Henry I. What is especially significant for the history of the Fitz Alans and, in turn, the Wallace family was that David I 'naturally identified improvement with adaptation to the Norman institutions he knew so well' (R.L.G. Ritchie, *The Normans in Scotland* [Edinburgh University, 1954]). His reign saw the introduction of Norman-French families into key positions in the Scottish royal household, and as a result Walter Fitz Alan was given the office of Steward as a hereditary position in about 1136. William Cumin became Chancellor of Scotland at about the same time after training as a clerk in Henry I's royal chancery. By 1140 Hugh Moreville had become royal Constable in Scotland. Other Norman families were brought into Scotland to fulfil specific roles. The Bruces, in the person of the first Robert Bruce, were presented by David I with the lordship of Annandale in south-west Scotland as early as 1124. This was to help the Scottish king define his authority in this area of Scotland, a notoriously separatist region. All of these Norman-French families were well rewarded with extensive landed possessions for their respective roles.

Walter Fitz Alan, being the first 'Stewart' in Scotland, was the originator of the Stewart 'empire' in Scotland. He served three successive Scottish kings, David I, Malcolm IV and William I, until his death in 1177. Professor G.W.S. Barrow has meticulously charted the build-up of this 'empire' in his books *The Anglo-Norman Era in Scottish History* (Oxford, Clarendon Press, 1980) and *The Kingdom of the Scots: Government, Church and Society from the Eleventh to the Fourteenth Century* (London, Edward Arnold, 1973), and much of the following section is derived from his work.

The chief base for the early Stewarts was Renfrewshire with Renfrew, its castle and burgh, at its heart. The Stewart presence here was consolidated in 1163 when Walter the Stewart founded a religious house of Cluniac monks brought from the Fitz Alan family's monastic foundation at Much Wenlock in Shropshire. In 1169, this religious community moved from Renfrew to the valley of the River Cart at Paisley. Paisley Abbey became the special 'family' monastery of the

Stewarts. Walter the first Stewart possessed a large part of the parish of Paisley. Apart from land in Renfrewshire and Lanarkshire, the early Stewarts had property in Ayrshire, especially Kyle Stewart. The main headquarters here was probably Dundonald with its castle. Other important centres in Ayrshire were Prestwick, Sanquhar, Tarbolton, Craigie and Riccarton. Other Stewart lands included territory in East Lothian, Roxburghshire and Berwickshire. Just as the Fitz Alans had benefited from the patronage of Henry I, so the new Scottish 'empire' of the Scottish branch of the Fitz Alan family (who became known as the Stewarts) was in turn able to give better prospects to a large number of their dependants and tenants. Professor Barrow has noted that a sizeable number of Fitz Alan henchmen came to Scotland from Shropshire and the Welsh marcher area – these included the Hosés from Albright Hussey, Robert of 'Montgomery', Robert Hunald from Marchamley, Stephen Kinnerley from Great or Little Ness and the Constantine family from Eaton Constantine. Within this group of Stewart dependants were the Wallace family.

The origins of the Wallace family are not known but the number of Wallaces to be found in twelfth-century Shropshire suggests that the investigation should begin there. The name is not a territorial name but a nickname meaning 'the Welshman'. It was written 'Walays' by William Wallace himself, 'le Waleys' by contemporaries. This does not, necessarily, indicate that the Wallaces were Welsh; it probably has a more general meaning 'from the Welsh marches'. Professor Barrow has tentatively suggested that the Wallace family may have been the same as the Ness family, i.e. the family called 'of Ness' (Great or Little Ness, Salop) There are strong resemblances between the personal names of the two families, both came to Scotland from Shropshire and were under the patronage of the early Stewarts. Such proof is not conclusive, however, and perhaps attention should focus more closely on the known links between the Wallaces and the Fitz Alans.

The first Wallace to be associated with the Fitz Alans was Richard 'le Waleys' (Wallace). Whether a Welshman or a borderer, he had been 'Normanised' by 1166 when he appears in the records as a paid sergeant-at-arms in Shropshire under William Fitz Alan, Lord of Oswestry. It seems that this Richard was in the Shropshire party of dependants who followed in the train of William Fitz Alan's brother, Walter, after he had been made Steward of the Scottish royal household in 1136. The date of Richard Wallace's move is not known but he was certainly there before 1174 when he appeared in Walter Stewart's entourage as a witness to Walter's grant to Paisley Abbey in that year. Richard seems to have been given land by the early Stewarts, either Walter or his successor, Alan, in Ayrshire. Richard or a successor, by the same name, held land as tenants of the Stewarts in the Sanquhar, Tarbolton and Mauchline areas of Kyle, Ayrshire. In view of

The Elderslie Yew. Local tradition claims that this ancient tree dates back to Wallace's time.

these contacts it seems probably that Riccarton (meaning Richard's 'tun' or 'manor') was named after Richard Wallace and was part of the original grant of Scottish lands to him by the first Walter Stewart. The first Wallace named William to appear in the records occurs in the context of other Stewart lands, on this occasion in East Lothian. In the time of the first Walter Stewart (died 1177) it is recorded that Robert of Stenton's rights in Stenton (East Lothian) passed to a William Wallace as husband of Robert's daughter, Isabel. Professor Barrow has found seven Wallaces associated with the first three Stewarts in the period up to 1241. Their names were Alan, Adam, Henry, Stephen, William and two Richards.

It is difficult to say whether the William Wallace of Stirling Bridge was descended from Richard Wallace or one of the other Wallaces mentioned above. It is within the context of Stewart landholding and the Stewart-Wallace relationship, developed from the second half of the twelfth century, that the early life of William Wallace must be assessed and the places associated with that life, perhaps, identified. The first site to be connected with William Wallace in historical record was Lanark where Wallace killed the English Sheriff of Lanark, whose jurisdiction may have covered some of Wallace's lands. Given the uncertainty over the name of William Wallace's father, it is no surprise that it is unclear where William Wallace was born and brought up. Tradition has made Riccarton the place of birth of William Wallace's father. Blind Harry associates William's father with the land 'of Ellerslie', which has long been accepted as Elderslie, near Paisley. Consequently Elderslie has been associated with William Wallace's birth, though there is no proof that his family held this area at the end of the thirteenth century. They did possess it by the late fourteenth century and it lay in the heart of Stewart country.

It is interesting to speculate, though this must remain conjecture, whether any of Blind Harry's tales of William Wallace's youthful adventures contain some geographically accurate family traditions. Certainly one story involved William Wallace in a clash with English soldiers while he was fishing in the River Irvine near Riccarton. In this episode Riccarton was the home of his Uncle Richard and it is mentioned several times in Blind Harry's story, indicating that it was a place of special family significance. Riccarton apart, Ayrshire generally is

Left: This plaque on the Elderslie Wallace Monument shows Wallace receiving the Guardianship of Scotland.

Right: The parish church at Riccarton. This town rivals Elderslie as the place most associated with William Wallace's early life.

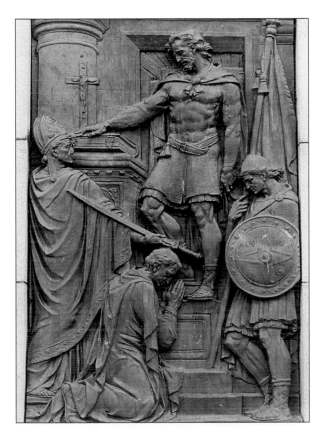

Irvine Water, Ayrshire. According to Blind Harry, William Wallace, while staying with another relative at Riccarton, became involved in a fight with English soldiers at Irvine Water where he was fishing.

important in Wallace's early activities, according to Blind Harry, with Ayr playing a key role. Wallace was apparently held prisoner at Ayr Castle for a while, and the infamous massacre of Scottish lords took place at the Barns of Ayr. These associations seem important in view of the known Stewart and Wallace connections in Ayrshire. If William Wallace's father was Alan 'Walays', this may have been the Alan 'Walays' described as a tenant of the King, of Ayrshire, whose homage to Edward I was recorded in August 1296. Elderslie, on the other hand, seems central to the Wallace homeland according to Blind Harry's testimony. As it was the focus of Stewart landownership in Renfrewshire this could add veracity to Blind Harry's tale too. Lanark is also given a link with Wallace's early life by Blind Harry's story of Wallace's mistress being situated there. This could have significance since Wallace's first generally accepted historical action in 1297, the murder of the English sheriff, William Hesilrigg, also took place at Lanark.

Yet there are other references made by Blind Harry to places involved in William Wallace's early life which seem to lack the same authenticity. M. McDiarmid, in his careful scrutiny of the text of Blind Harry's *The Wallace*, notes the oddity of so many references to Wallace's links outside western Scotland – that Wallace had an uncle in the Carse of Gowrie who had helped in his upbringing before he was sent to Dundee for his education, and Kilspindie (Perthshire) is given a specific mention here; that another relative, a parson, gave him temporary dwelling at Dunipace (Stirlingshire); that he had a mistress at Perth; that Wallace's mother took refuge at one stage in Dunfermline Abbey. All of these links seem rather improbable without supporting evidence. Paisley Abbey rather than Dundee seems a more likely place for Wallace to have been educated. McDiarmid has pointed out that some of the detail in the poem may reflect Harry's own environment and contacts and, perhaps, his own education. He concludes that as a writer Harry deliberately slanted the story of William Wallace to the environment known to himself and a series of family friends and contacts that he wished to compliment by including them in his tale. As a result, perhaps, areas between the firths of Forth and Tay, especially their inner reaches, i.e. north-east Stirlingshire, Linlithgow, south-east Perthshire, north-west Fife and south-west Angus,

A good impression of the Seal of William Wallace used in 1297 on the letter Wallace and Andrew Moray sent to Lübeck and Hamburg; the original is housed in Lübeck. The legend around the seal seems to read 'Willelmi le Waleys filii Alani' (William Wallace son of Alan). If Wallace's father was Alan Walays, this was probably the Alan Walays, tenant of the King, of Ayrshire, whose homage to Edward I was recorded in August 1296. This seems to confirm details of William Wallace's Ayrshire origins. The bow symbol on the seal would seem to be a sign of Wallace's non-noble origins. (By courtesy of the Mitchell Library, Glasgow.)

Cambuskenneth Abbey, near Dunipace, where Wallace, according to Blind Harry, lived with his uncle, a cleric. There is also a tradition that one of Wallace's arms was buried at the abbey.

Kilspindie church. Blind Harry, again, records how William Wallace was taken by his mother to stay with an uncle at Kilspindie (between Perth and Dundee). Apparently, Wallace received early education at Dundee.

SITE OF CASTLE OF DUNDEE
DESTROYED *CIR* 1314 — NEAR THIS SPOT
WILLIAM WALLACE STRUCK THE FIRST BLOW
FOR SCOTTISH INDEPENDENCE *CIR* 1288
HERE WAS THE BIRTHPLACE OF
ADMIRAL DUNCAN 1731
VICTOR OF CAMPERDOWN 1797
IN HOUSE ADJOINING
THE CHEVALIER DE ST. GEORGE
SPENT THE NIGHT OF 6TH JANUARY 1716
AFTER PUBLIC ENTRY INTO DUNDEE

The plaque at Dundee. This refers to an incident in Blind Harry's account of one of Wallace's first encounters with the English at Dundee. There is no historical record of Wallace's connection with Dundee until 1297 when he was actively involved in besieging the town.

receive rather more attention than would be expected considering the Wallaces' family and feudal connections in western Scotland.

It is difficult to separate Wallace family traditions from Blind Harry's personal affectations as a writer. Yet it is necessary to delve into William Wallace's obscure family origins and background to try to find the answer to a key historical question. Was Wallace an independent adventurer spurred into military action against the English in 1297 by wrongs committed against his family and friends or was he simply a loyal 'frontman' carrying out the orders of feudal overlords, the Stewarts?

John of Fordun implied that William Wallace was already in hiding or perhaps an outlaw when he killed the English Sheriff of Lanark: 'William lifted up his head from his den.' The rather more numerous contemporary English sources, as well as making disparaging remarks about Wallace's family background, are unanimous in referring to him as a criminal in their first references. To the Guisborough chronicler he was '. . . a common thief', 'a public robber', 'a vagrant fugitive . . . who had been outlawed many times'. To the Lanercost chronicler Wallace was 'a bloody man who had formerly been a leader of brigands'. To the anonymous author of *Song*

Wallace's mother is said to have been buried in the churchyard of Dunfermline Abbey. A plaque now commemorates her life.

on the Scottish Wars he was 'a robber'. To Peter Langtoft Wallace was 'the master of thieves', while to Matthew of Westminster he was 'a robber given to sacrilege'. To William Rishanger Wallace was 'an expert archer who made his living by bow and quiver', implying, perhaps, the life of an outlaw. Finally, in the Royal Manuscript Wallace was a 'peasant rascal from nowhere'. If, as seems probable, William Wallace was already a criminal before he murdered the English sheriff in 1297, what were the circumstances behind this outlawry and was it connected with the actions of William Heselrigg, Sheriff of Lanark and Clydesdale?

Tradition established by the two fifteenth-century sources Andrew Wyntoun and Blind Harry states that the young William Wallace had a confrontation with a group of English troops in Lanark. English soldiers formed an army of occupation in key centres of southern Scotland following the disastrous defeat of the Scottish

A window at Dunfermline Abbey.

MARGARET MOTHER OF WILLIAM WALLACE LIES BURIED BENEATH THORN TREE IN THE GROUNDS OF DUNFERMLINE ABBEY

The Abbot's House plaque at Dunfermline Abbey. Another memorial to William Wallace's mother and her traditional association with Dunfermline Abbey.

army at Dunbar on 27 April 1296, when an estimated 10,000 Scots (undoubtedly an exaggeration) died. Wallace, though outnumbered, inflicted heavy casualties among the soldiers before fleeing to his 'lemman' or mistress – Harry named her as Marion Braidfute and described her as Wallace's wife. She was eventually captured and executed on the orders of William Heselrigg, Sheriff of Lanark. This story may explain Wallace's act of vengeance. However, there is no supporting evidence for the existence of Marion Braidfute, whose name, it has been suggested, was suspiciously close to the family name of one of Blind Harry's neighbours. This account also does not explain Wallace's probable status as an outlaw before the event.

Both Andrew Wyntoun and Blind Harry mention the hardship and suffering of the Wallace family itself. Wyntoun states:

> Willame Walays in Clyddysdale,
> That saw hys kyn supprysyd hale

Blind Harry refers to the scattering of the Wallace family:

The ruins of the parish church of St Kentigern, Lanark, where, tradition has it, Wallace married Marion Braidfute.

The Norman doorway at Lamington church. Lamington is an estate on the Clyde with a castle, the remains of which mainly consist of a tower house. Lamington is associated with the Wallace tradition through William Wallace's wife or mistress, Marion Braidfute, heiress of Lamington. This doorway would have been present in Wallace's time though there is no documentary evidence, only myth, to connect him with the site.

> For at this time Scotland was almost lost,
> And overspread with a rude South'ron host.
> Wallace's father to the Lennox fled
> His eldest son he thither with him led . . .
> To Ellerslie he and his mother went,
> She on the morrow for her brother sent,
> Who told her, to her sorrow, grief and pain,
> Her husband and her eldest son were slain

It is feasible that William Wallace's villain status prior to 1297 may have been related to some of the Wallace family's refusal to swear fealty to Edward I following his twenty-one-week victory march around Scotland after the Battle of Dunbar. Edward I gathered the fealties of all landholders of substance in Scotland, who, by so doing, acknowledged his position as overlord of Scotland, and these were collected in a document known as

Tinto viewed from Lamington. This is an area associated, by Blind Harry, with the courtship and relationship of William Wallace and Marion Braidfute, who was, apparently, heiress of Lamington, which is 12 miles from Lanark.

the 'Ragman Roll'. Over 1,500 landowners between May and August 1296 swore:

> I will be faithful and loyal and will bear fealty and loyalty to King Edward, king of England and his heirs . . . and will never bear arms nor give counsel nor help to anyone against him nor his heirs, whatever should happen in the future, with the help of God and the Saints . . .

It has been remarked that William Wallace's name was not on the list of those pledging their allegiance to Edward and that this explains his outlaw standing in 1297. Wallace, perhaps, as a younger son did not have sufficient status as a property owner to appear on the list. However, there is no sign either of William's known elder brother Malcolm or the elder brother Andrew named in Bower's *Scotichronicon*. There are some Wallace names in the 'Ragman Roll' – Adam and Alan (two names associated with the Stewart lordship earlier in the thirteenth century), John la Wallace Fitz Thomas le Wallace (noted as being from the country of Fife) and a Nicol le Wallace as well as a John le Wallace of Over Etone. If Alan Wallace, of Ayrshire, was the father of William Wallace it is possible that William Wallace's homage, as a younger man, may have been deemed unnecessary. John of Fordun implied that William Wallace's father had died just prior to 1297 and that William's elder brother (named Andrew by Walter Bower) had 'inherited a landed estate'. Of course, he would not be allowed to succeed to the estate if he had not submitted to the new English regime in 1296.

Perhaps property and inheritance is at the heart of William Wallace's complaint against Heselrigg in 1297, a grievance liable to be more fierce if either Wallace's father and/or elder brother had been slain, as claimed by both Andrew Wyntoun and Blind Harry. Heselrigg's jurisdiction in the sheriffdom of Lanark would include both the organisation of fealty-taking as well as property matters and he was apparently holding local assizes in Lanark when the attack by William Wallace and his men took place.

That William Wallace was already a man on the run in 1297, suggested by Fordun, incorporated into a more detailed account of his family's hardships by Andrew Wyntoun and Blind Harry and fervently argued by all contemporary English chroniclers, is given extra weight by a Scottish legal record of 8 August 1296 which refers to a 'William le Waleys, thief'. This document accuses 'William Waleys, thief' in his absence of assisting a renegade priest, Matthew of York, to rob Cristiana of St John (Perth) at her house in Perth and taking by force beer to the value of 3s

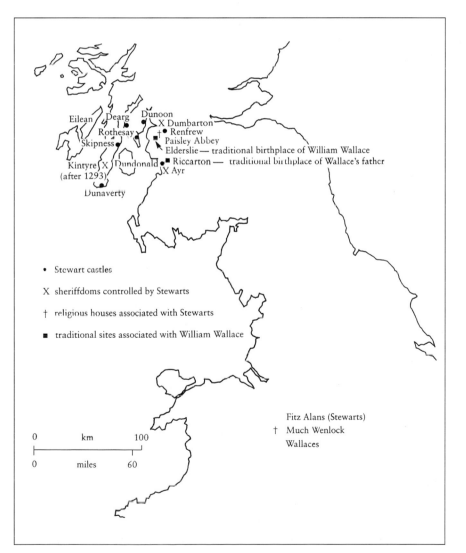

Wallace and the Stewarts.

Glasgow Cathedral. Robert Wishart, Bishop of Glasgow, played a major part in supporting Scottish resistance to the English. He backed Wallace and was a major source of assistance to Robert Bruce's coup in 1306. Wishart was buried here.

(approximately 36 gallons by modern prices). The date of the offence is given as Thursday next before St Botulph's Day, i.e. June 1296. This would fit in with the notion that Wallace and some of his family fled from his home area in the aftermath of the English victory against the Scottish army at Dunbar on 27 April and the subsequent attempt, sheriffdom by sheriffdom, to extract oaths of fealty from landowners. The place of the robbery also tallies with the many adventures of William Wallace in this area described by Blind Harry, which, as has been seen, would otherwise appear to lack historical substance.

The legend-making of Bower, Wyntoun and particularly Blind Harry naturally concentrate attention on William Wallace himself and his family and perhaps give the impression of an individual adventurer acting either on his own behalf or that of his family. This approach does not set William Wallace's motivation in the wider context of the Wallaces' overlords, the Stewart family, or indeed the broader political interests of that major landowning family. Those English chroniclers who are held in respect for their detailed contemporary commentary on the Scottish wars, such as the Lanercost and Guisborough chroniclers, suggest two leaders of the Scottish nobility as being the principal initiators of the 1297 revolt against the English. James Stewart (*c.* 1260–1309) was certainly one of the main leaders in 1297. To the Lanercost chronicler, the issue was clear-cut:

> . . . [the Bishop of Glasgow, Robert Wishart] conspired with the Steward of the realm, named James for a new piece of insolence . . . Not daring openly to break their pledged faith to the king, they caused a certain bloody man, William Wallace, who had formerly been chief of brigands in Scotland, to revolt against the king and assemble the people in his support . . .

What were the Stewarts' motives, especially after their very rapid submission to Edward I after the Battle of Dunbar?

As has already been said, the Stewart family had established themselves as a powerful landowning family by 1200 as a result of grants of property from Scottish kings. The growth in their landed fortunes continued throughout the thirteenth century and was consolidated particularly in the west. James Stewart, the head of the Stewart family at the time of William Wallace, had inherited the family's lordships in Renfrewshire and Ayrshire but also had gained new Stewart land in Bute and Cowal, acquired in the thirteenth century. A younger member of the family, Walter, had received the earldom of Menteith in about 1260. With greater landed possessions came political offices and more power. Walter, Earl of

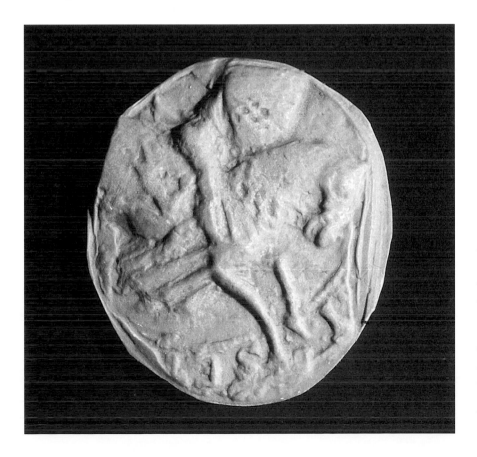

The Seal of James Stewart (*c.* 1260–1309), the overlord of William Wallace, which dates from about 1270. Obverse: Stewart is depicted on horseback to sinister, in armour with lance and shield bearing arms. The horse is armorially caparisoned. The seal is incomplete. (By permission of the Court of the Lord Lyon.)

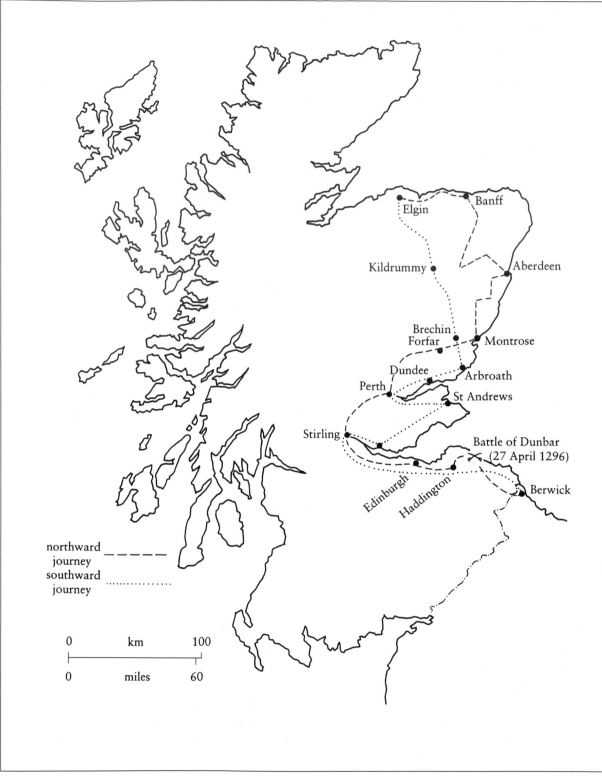

Edward I's invasion of Scotland, 1296.

Menteith was Sheriff of Ayr by 1264 and Sheriff of Dumbarton between 1271 and 1288; he was also prominent in royal witness lists. Alexander Stewart and his son, James, were regularly seen in the royal circle after 1260. James Stewart was Sheriff of Ayr in 1288 and Sheriff of Dumbarton in 1289. The Stewarts exercised their influence, political, military and economic, through a series of private castles – Renfrew, Rothesay, Dundonald and Dunoon, and perhaps also Glassary and Eilean Dearg. Their control over the royal castles at Ayr and Dumbarton through the offices of sheriff (still held in 1292) consolidated their power in the west. Under the kingship of John Balliol (1292–6), James Stewart was further bolstered when the 1293 Parliament sought to establish a new sheriffdom, of Kintyre, under his authority. This comprised Bute, the Cumbraes, Kintyre and probably Arran and both complemented and extended Stewart authority in this region. Stewart control over the entire Firth of Clyde zone would have been dominant if the scheme of 1293 had been put in force. Even without this, James Stewart was in charge of Kintyre at the beginning of the Scottish wars and had either Skipness or Dunaverty as his chief castle in the region.

The motive of James Stewart in submitting to Edward I only sixteen days after the English victory at Dunbar was surely to preserve Stewart family dominance in western Scotland. Edward I sought to ensure Stewart loyalty to his overlordship by arranging a marriage alliance between James Stewart and the sister of one of Edward's closest supporters, Burgh, Earl of Ulster. It seemed at first that Edward was willing to use Stewart to help him control Scotland – James Stewart was soon employed to receive the surrender of the Comyn castle of Kirkintilloch on about 10 June. However, James Stewart's political supremacy in western Scotland soon came under threat by Edward I's new English appointments. In September 1296 Henry Percy was appointed English Warden of Ayr and Galloway. In the north-west, Edward attempted to extend English influence by appointing Alexander Macdonald of Islay as Baillie of Kintyre, a position formerly under James Stewart's jurisdiction. Between April and September 1296 Stewart gradually came to see that he would be deprived of most of his political control (and power) in the west of Scotland by two of Edward I's new agents. James Stewart had a lot to lose from the English government in Scotland.

Both James Stewart and William Wallace had their reasons for revolting against the English overlordship of Scotland and the means used to secure it. Only analysis of their action in 1297 will assist us in understanding whether Wallace was an independent adventurer or merely a 'frontman' for his Stewart lords.

3

WILLIAM WALLACE AND THE REVOLT OF 1297

The actions of William Wallace and his lord, James Stewart, in 1297 need to be set in the context of the Anglo-Scottish war, which began so disastrously for Scotland with the defeat at Dunbar in 1296. Their roles should also be examined against the background of the Scottish political community, its leadership and its policy in 1296. The Scots were led into war in 1296 by the Comyn family, who had dominated Scottish politics and landholding for much of the thirteenth century. The two main branches of the family, the Comyn lords of Badenoch and Lochaber and the Comyn earls of Buchan, controlled key castles and therefore the main lines of communication, especially in northern Scotland where their virtually vice-regal power stretched from Inverlochy Castle in the west to Slains Castle in the east. Between these two points they had in their power strategically situated castles at Ruthven, Lochindorb, Blair Atholl, Balvenie, Dundarg, Cairnbulg (originally called Philorth), Rattray and Kingedward. In particular, Comyn strongholds controlled important passes from the north and west Highlands into the Tay basin.

However, Comyn power was not only restricted to northern Scotland. The family, including a third branch – the Comyns of Kilbride – had a great deal of land and power in central and southern Scotland. They held castles at Kirkintilloch (Dumbartonshire), Dalswinton (Nithsdale), Cruggleton (Galloway), Bedrule and Scraesburgh (Roxburghshire) and Kilbride (East Kilbride). In addition to their private landholding, the Comyns controlled a number of royal castles through their role as hereditary sheriffs of Dingwall and Banff (in the north) and Wigtown (in the south-west). In the early 1290s the family took additional responsibility for the royal castles at Kirkcudbright, Aberdeen, Jedburgh, Clunie, Dull and Brideburgh (Barburgh in Dumfriesshire). Comyn influence over the political scene was further enhanced by marriage alliances in the course of the thirteenth century with the earls of Mar, Ross, Dunbar, Angus, Strathearn and Fife and with the powerful families of Macdougall, Moray, Balliol, Mowbray, Umphraville and Soules. Other prominent allies were the Grahams, Frasers, Sinclairs, Cheynes, Mowats, Lochores, Maxwells and Hays. The Comyns, therefore, with their wide-ranging and extensive landed power and their network of powerful partners exercised political influence at the centre as well as in many regions of Scotland. Their long-standing authority was witnessed by their extended tenure of the Justiciarship of Scotia, the most important political and administrative office in the kingdom – three successive Comyn earls of Buchan were justiciars of Scotia for no fewer than sixty-six years between about 1205 and 1304.

In the context of this network of well-established noble ruling families, it is interesting to place the families of Stewart and Bruce. It is clear that the Stewarts were not within the Comyn network of allies who so dominated Scottish government. However, it would appear that the Stewarts were part of the aristocratic group upon which Alexander III depended to consolidate royal authority in the regions. The Stewarts, with their hereditary role as 'Steward' guaranteeing them a role in the royal circle, moved firmly to the forefront of Scotland's political community with their extensive landholding in the west of Scotland, recognised and further consolidated by control of the sheriffdoms of Ayr and Dumbarton. The family were prominent in the royal circle from the 1250s to the 1280s. The Bruces, on the other hand, held no political offices in Alexander III's reign. However, their status and landholding power in Scotland had been increased in 1272 when the family gained the earldom of Carrick in south-west Scotland, and this built on their existing strength in this area, which was based upon the lordship of Annandale they had held since 1124. The Bruces, though outside the political elite of noble families in Alexander III's reign, did have much ambition and a dormant claim to the Scottish throne – apparently acknowledged by Alexander II in 1238 and by the Scottish baronage in the late 1240s – should the male line of the Scottish royal family die out. It is in this light that the Stewarts' family connections with the Bruces should be noted. A marriage between Walter Fitz Alan II and Euphemia, daughter of William Bruce and sister of Robert Bruce, indicates that these links dated from 1261.

The Stewarts' role at the centre of Scottish government as well as their family links with the Bruces were both emphasised in the dramatic events of 1286. On 18 March 1286, Alexander III, King of Scots, died suddenly, aged forty-four, the result of a tragic accident on a dark, stormy night when he was on his way to Kinghorn to meet his new French wife (of less than six months), Yolande de Dreux. There was great uncertainty over the succession. Yolande, Alexander III's queen was, at first, believed to be pregnant, though the magnates of Scotland had acknowledged the 'Maid of Norway', Alexander III's granddaughter, Margaret (then aged one), as rightful heir in February 1284 should Alexander III not produce an heir.

Overleaf, background image:
Bywell Castle on the River Tyne.

JOHN BALLIOL

The names of William Wallace and Robert Bruce have captured popular imagination and hold a unique place in Scottish history and tradition. In contrast, that of John Balliol has been associated with the abject surrender of his kingdom to Edward I in 1296. Balliol acquired the derogatory nickname of 'Toom Tabard' ('Empty Surcoat') after his coat of royal arms was stripped from his tabard in public and humiliating circumstances following his formal submission to Edward I at Montrose on 8 July 1296. As the main opponent of the Bruces' dynastic ambitions in the 'Great Cause' (1291–2), John Balliol has naturally been given a 'bad press' by the pro-Bruce Scottish writers of the fourteenth and

The Great Seal of John Balliol, King of Scots, c. 1295. Reverse: the King on horseback to sinister, in chain mail, with loose-flowing sleeveless tunic, crowned helmet with grated front and slits for sight, a sword in his right hand and a large shield suspended from his shoulders bearing arms. There is a lion rampant with a royal tressure. The horse has similar arms on its caparisons, which are quite rigid and entirely cover the tail, while the hoofs have spiked shoes. The legend reads: 'IOHANNES DEI GRACIA REX SCOTTORUM' (John, by God's grace, King of the Scots). There are fleurs-de-lis between the words. (By permission of the Court of the Lord Lyon.)

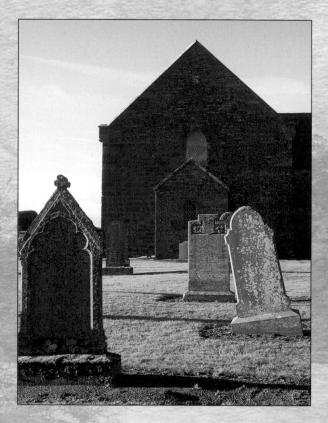

Stracathro church. After the Scottish defeat at the Battle of Dunbar in April 1296, John Balliol (who was probably not present) fled to the north with his main supporters, the Comyns. The Comyns, the real leaders of the Scottish political community, decided to seek surrender terms during the summer. In early July 1296, Balliol submitted to Edward I at Stracathro church, north of Brechin, before proceeding to Montrose where he was forced to give up his crown.

Barnard Castle, the principal English stronghold of the Balliol family (their other northern base was Bywell in Northumberland). Barnard Castle received significant additions in the second half of the thirteenth century, a reflection of the family's wealth at this time.

Sweetheart Abbey, Nithsdale. Probably not completed before the outbreak of the Scottish wars, Sweetheart Abbey was founded in 1273 by the rich and pious Devorguilla Balliol in honour of her husband, John (died 1268). Devorguilla was the mother of John Balliol, King of Scots, 1292–6.

fifteenth centuries. To Walter Bower (*c.* 1440) the Scottish kingdom was 'abnormal in the time of this disastrous King John'. This was in keeping with the official government propaganda of the Bruce kingship, which in 1308 referred to itself as the successor to Alexander III (ignoring any reference to John Balliol's kingship) and in 1309 (for the first time) declared that Balliol had been imposed by English force on the Scots. Despite Balliol's lack of political experience and personal frailties, it should be remembered that the Scots fought in his name and on his behalf from 1296 onwards. He symbolised Scottish independence for William Wallace between 1297 and 1305. Even after Robert Bruce's 'coup' of 1306, Balliol remained a significant focus for opposition to Robert Bruce until his death in 1313, after which his son Edward Balliol continued to represent Balliol interests. The Bruces still needed to wage a propaganda war even after Bannockburn.

As a result of the confusion and the inevitability of a long period of minority government, a provisional government of six Wardens or Guardians was set up. This comprised two earls (Alexander Comyn, Earl of Buchan, and Duncan, Earl of Fife), two bishops (William Fraser of St Andrews and Robert Wishart of Glasgow) and two barons (John Comyn of Badenoch and James Stewart). The *Lanercost Chronicle*'s description of this group as 'guardians of peace' highlights its key function: to maintain peace and stability within the kingdom and protect freedom from external interference. The Guardians were also in a good position to implement the succession and help to establish the next heir to either Yolande's child or Margaret, a delicate child of three years at the time of Alexander III's death. The two families considered to have the best claims to be heir presumptive were the Balliols and the Bruces. However, the Comyns dominated the Guardianship and had a strong family link to the Balliols – John Comyn, Lord of Badenoch (died 1302) was the brother-in-law of John Balliol, the Balliol candidate and eventual King of Scots in 1292. These factors persuaded the Bruces to resort to strong-arm tactics in 1286, and they launched attacks on the Balliol castle at Buittle and the royal castles of Wigtown and Dumfries.

The potential for a clash of allegiances for James Stewart, and his following, was clearly present in 1286. The Turnberry Band of September 1286 seemed to indicate that the Stewarts were putting family loyalty before national interests. The pact made at Turnberry (the chief castle of the Bruce earldom of Carrick) linked Robert Bruce, Lord of Annandale (a potential claimant to the Scottish throne and the future Robert I's grandfather), his son Robert Bruce, Earl of Carrick, James Stewart (the Guardian), his brother, John Stewart of Jedburgh, Walter Stewart, Earl of Menteith, and his sons, Patrick, Earl of Dunbar, Angus Macdonald, Lord of Islay, and his son in an agreement to support Richard Burgh, Earl of Ulster, and Thomas Clare against their enemies. This involved swearing oaths of allegiance to the English King and whoever should be King in Scotland 'by reason of the blood of the lord Alexander, king of Scotland, according to the ancient customs hitherto approved and used in the Kingdom of Scotland'. The oath has been interpreted as an indication of a deliberate bid by the Bruces, supported by their close family allies, the Stewarts, for the Scottish throne. This is, probably, reading too much into the statement and there may have been nothing more to the agreement than a family/factional pact to conquer land in the west of Ireland. Yet, at a time of uncertainty following the death of Alexander III, when disorder in south-west Scotland was being initiated by the Bruces, any military pact such as that at Turnberry must have been viewed with suspicion by the Comyn-led government and their allies.

James Stewart, despite the Stewart family's support for the Bruces at Turnberry, tended to put his duties as Guardian before the concerns of his partners within Scotland. He backed, for example, the Guardians' policy of putting the host on twenty-four hours' readiness to suppress unrest. Perhaps the Stewarts felt that their interests in the south-west and west were threatened by the Bruces' strong-arm actions, which could have turned that area into a civil-war zone. It is difficult to assess the individual role of James Stewart within the six-man team of Guardians between 1286 and 1290. Evidence suggests that he supported the collective policy decisions of the committee but did not play a leading part in their active implementation. Stewart was not a member of, for instance, either of the two embassies dispatched to Edward I in France during the summer of 1286 to receive his counsel and perhaps ask for his help to bring stability to the Scottish political scene.

In 1289 the committee of Guardians was reduced to four by the deaths of Alexander Comyn, Earl of Buchan, and Duncan, Earl of Fife. Despite this, James Stewart maintained his low-key role, for example, in the negotiations for a marriage between Margaret, 'Maid of Norway', the Scottish heiress, and Edward I's heir, Edward of Caernarfon. He was not one of the Guardians who arranged the Treaty of Salisbury (1289) with the English representatives; nor was he involved in the discussions for bringing the young Scottish heiress from Norway to Scotland in 1290. Stewart was not regarded as a member of the dominating Comyn clique who tended to control membership of missions and embassies implementing Guardian policy. Undoubtedly, the Comyns were suspicious of the Stewarts' association with the Bruces, openly displayed in 1286, while appreciating the need to acknowledge the importance of Stewart authority in the west in order to maintain stability in that area. It can only be surmised that Stewart followers, such as the Wallace family, shared Stewart ambivalence in a difficult political climate. The Stewarts could not afford to lose their position in central and local government which consolidated their power and influence in western Scotland, yet their family connection with the Bruces must have caused some tension with the dominant Comyn family.

The position of the Stewarts in the network of influential noble families is important for understanding the factors that affected William Wallace and his family. Another important consideration is the policy and political stance adopted by Scotland's aristocratic governing community in the ten years between the death of Alexander III in 1286 and the outbreak of the Anglo–Scottish wars in 1296. The tendency of Scottish tradition – the foundations of which were firmly laid by the writings of John Barbour (writing in about 1375), John of Fordun (1380s), Andrew Wyntoun (c. 1420), Walter Bower (c. 1440) and Blind Harry (c. 1470s) – has been to emphasise the factiousness of a nobility whose motivation was self-interest rather than the national interest. This served to highlight the roles of William Wallace and Robert Bruce as champions of Scottish nationalism, the only clear embodiments of a policy of Scottish independence against English imperialism. This distorted view, from the fourteenth and fifteenth centuries, has hidden the reality that a definite political focus did emerge in the period after Alexander III's death. The negotiations for the marriage between Margaret, 'Maid of Norway', and Edward of Caernarfon culminated in the Treaty of Birgham (eventually signed in July 1290), which embodied a detailed and carefully considered expression of the Scottish government's position on Scottish rights and Scottish independence. Scotland had a defined political manifesto and a distinct sense of its own identity before William Wallace (in 1297) and Robert Bruce (in 1306) came to dominate the Scottish political scene. The following extract is taken from the Treaty of Birgham:

. . . the realm of Scotland shall remain separated, apart and free in itself, without subjection to the realm of England, by its rightful boundaries and marches, as it has been preserved down to the present . . . the rights, laws, liberties and customs of the same realm of Scotland to be preserved in every respect and in all time coming throughout the said realm and its borders, completely and without being impaired . . . The relics, charters, privileges and other muniments which concern the royal dignity and the realm of Scotland shall be deposited in a secure place within the realm of Scotland, under strong guard, under the seals of the greatest magnates of the realm and under their supervision . . . Parliament shall not be held outwith the realm of Scotland or its marches to deal with these matters which concern that realm or its marches, or to deal with the status of the inhabitants within that realm. No tallages, aids, military service of maltols [an arbitrary tax on exports, imports or internal markets] shall be demanded from the aforesaid realm, or be imposed upon the people of the same realm, unless it be to meet the common needs of the realm and in circumstances in which the kings of Scots have been used to demand such things . . .

The leaders of the Scottish political community, including James Stewart, steadfastly pursued the key terms of the Treaty of Birgham. These elements became the backbone of the Scottish fight for independence when this was threatened by the death of the Scottish

Norham Castle, the chief border stronghold of the Bishop of Durham. It was appropriate that Edward I stayed here – Anthony Bek, Bishop of Durham, was his chief adviser on Scottish affairs – while hearing the claims of the thirteen Competitors for the Scottish throne in 1291.

heiress, the 'Maid of Norway', in Orkney late in September 1290 as she made her way to Scotland. Edward I had been taking an increasingly interventionist stance towards Scotland even before the Treaty of Birgham and this became accentuated after the death of the 'Maid of Norway'. It is important to trace the development of this approach in the years prior to William Wallace's emergence in 1297. As early as February 1290, for example, Edward I granted to Anthony Bek, Bishop of Durham, the custody of the lands and tenements in Cumberland and Northumberland which had formerly been held by the King of Scotland. Later, in June 1290, the custody of the Isle of Man, clearly a part of the Scottish kingdom, was given to Walter Hunterscumbe. While the position adopted by the Scottish Guardians in the terms of the Treaty of Birgham (July 1290) could be viewed as a response to incipient English encroachment, Edward I still reserved some rights for himself in this treaty:

> We reserve to our aforesaid lord, and to any other person, such right, concerning matters on the border or elsewhere, as may have belonged to them prior to the date of this present grant, or which could rightfully belong to them in the future . . . by reason of this present treaty nothing shall be added to, nor taken away from, the right of either realm . . .

In August 1290, Edward I asked the Guardians of Scotland to recognise Anthony Bek, Bishop of Durham, as the Lieutenant in Scotland of his son, Edward, and of his future wife, Margaret. The Guardians were then instructed to defer to Bek in matters 'which are required for the governance and peaceful state of the realm'.

Despite the promises made at Birgham that Scotland's independence would be safeguarded, the English attitude was increasingly clear – Scotland could only be stable politically with Edward I's oversight. English policy following the demise of the Scottish heiress (and, therefore, the marriage contract with Edward I's son) was to have English claims for overlordship over Scotland formally acknowledged in return for his assistance in securing the royal succession in Scotland and resisting the aggressive tactics of the Bruces, which again threatened the country with civil war. In keeping with the terms of the Treaty of Birgham, the Scottish Guardians at first refused to acknowledge Edward I's claims to overlordship. The King, however, cleverly outflanked the Guardians by getting the thirteen claimants to the Scottish throne to recognise that he was their rightful overlord and, as such, could oversee the process by which the Scottish succession would be decided. The spirit of Birgham was still present, however, and Edward had to concede that he would maintain the customary laws and liberties of the kingdom until a decision about the rightful king was made. Significantly, Robert Wishart, Bishop of

King John Balliol swears homage and fealty to Edward I. Edward I felt that he had the means to control King John after he had sworn homage and fealty to him on 26 December 1292 in most unambiguous terms. The stern look on Edward's face here was matched by a firm intention to define his overlordship to suit his own wishes. (Reproduced by permission of the British Library [Royal MS 20e vii f. 28].)

Glasgow, one of the Guardians and a close ally of James Stewart, rejected Edward I's claim to suzerainty. In addition, some, and perhaps all, of the Scottish royal castle commanders refused at first to hand over their castles to Edward on the grounds that they had been entrusted to their custody by Alexander III or the Guardians, not by the English King. James Stewart, himself, held the castles of Ayr and Dumbarton at this time.

These signs of resistance to full English overlordship turned out to be brief, however, for in June 1291 the Guardians felt they had no option but to agree to surrender Scottish royal castles; they also resigned their positions to be reappointed by the English King. They were no longer 'elected by the community' but now 'appointed by the most serene prince, the Lord Edward'. There then followed a general swearing of fealty to Edward I by all substantial freeholders, both lay and clerical. James Stewart, Robert Wishart and Sir Nicholas Segrave were appointed commissioners at Ayr to supervise the receipt of the fealties for western Scotland. Edward I clearly recognised the authority of Stewart, sheriff of both Ayr and Dumbarton, in western Scotland.

In August the court appointed by Edward I to decide which of the thirteen claimants or 'Competitors' had the best right to the Scottish throne met for the first time – the lawsuit that came to be known as the 'Great Cause' in the eighteenth century had begun. It was acknowledged at the time that the two most serious candidates were John Balliol and Robert Bruce (grandfather of the future king). As part of the process, Bruce was allowed to nominate forty auditors supporting his candidature, with Balliol and John Comyn (a relative as well as a Competitor) together nominating another forty in their support. The list of auditors is instructive. Again, James Stewart and Robert Wishart, Bishop of Glasgow, are positioned prominently among the Bruce auditors, which also include other families associated with the Stewarts such as the Lindsays and Crawfords. The Balliol and Comyn collection of auditors represents families that had been long associated with the Comyn family in government. The fact that Balliol was the official 'ruling party' candidate is emphasised by the Comyns' conduct of their own claims through John Comyn of Badenoch, the Competitor. Comyn withdrew his claim saying specifically that he did not want to prejudice the claims of John Balliol, his brother-in-law.

The final judgement in favour of John Balliol, based on superior legal strength by the principles of primogeniture of the Balliol cause, took place on 17 November 1292 and Balliol was enthroned on St Andrew's Day, 1292. It should be noted that Robert Wishart and James Stewart had both been determined and outspoken in support of the Bruce cause, though they had to accept the final judgement.

In terms of the Scottish government under John Balliol's kingship, it is hardly surprising that there was continuity in both personnel and policy with the time of the Guardianship. The dominance of the Comyn party continued. Judging from their appearance in the royal circle, the leading secular figures in the Balliol administration were John Comyn, Earl of Buchan, John Comyn II, Lord of Badenoch, Alexander Balliol, Geoffrey Mowbray and Patrick Graham. These men seemed to be the inner core of advisers most frequently involved at the centre of government. James Stewart retained his important role in the administration of western Scotland despite his strong support of the Bruce candidature for the Scottish throne. His role in the west was, in fact, increased during the first Parliament of Balliol's kingship in February 1293. An ordinance in this Parliament sought the establishment of three new sheriffdoms in Lorn, Skye and Kintyre in order to provide a permanent solution to the problem of royal authority in the north and west. The sheriffdom of Kintyre, comprising Bute, the Cumbraes, Kintyre and probably Arran, would be under the authority of James Stewart, adding to his offices of sheriff of both Dumbarton and Ayr.

Stewart backing for the Bruces was still apparent, however. With another Bruce ally, the Earl of Mar, James Stewart supported the confirmation of Robert Bruce, the future King, as Earl of Carrick at the Stirling Parliament of August 1293. This was despite the fact that Bruce's father and grandfather refused to do homage to John Balliol as Scottish

King. It seems that the youngest Robert Bruce must have done homage to Balliol – he was still hoping to press Bruce claims to power in Scotland. The Bruces were not the main danger to the Scottish government in 1292. Stewart, as an important member of this government, must have been aware of the threats posed to that body, and therefore his role in it, by an increasingly interventionist approach by Edward I. As soon as judgement had been made in favour of Balliol's claim to the Scottish throne, there was, apparently, a warning that if he did not rule justly Edward would have to intervene.

Only one week after John Balliol's enthronement, on 7 December 1292, Roger Bartholomew, a Berwick burgess, complained to Edward about three adverse judgements of the Guardians. Edward's rapid response – compensation payments were made by 6 January 1293 – indicated his desire to demonstrate his right to hear pleas. This drew an appeal from the leaders of the Scottish political community, represented by John Comyn, Earl of Buchan, Bishop William Fraser of St Andrews, Patrick Graham and Thomas Randulph – again neither Bishop Robert Wishart of Glasgow nor James Stewart were leading players. This, on behalf of their King, objected to Edward I making judgement outside Scotland and asked that the English King should keep the promises made in the Treaty of Birgham. Edward I's response was unambiguous: he had the right to review their decisions as the Guardians were, after June 1291, responsible to him alone as their overlord; any promises made by Edward in the interregnum, i.e. their Guardianship, were for that time alone and were no longer binding. Very early in Balliol's kingship, Edward was seeking to define his overlordship in a steadily more opportunistic way. The English King expressed the forcible viewpoint that he could hear whatever pleas might be brought to him, that he could, if necessary, summon the Scottish King, himself, and that, as far as appeals were concerned, he would not be bound by any previous promises that he had made.

Given these early indications of Edward I's severe definition of his overlordship of Scotland, as well as the government's increasingly desperate attempts to cling on to the principles of Scottish independence established at the Treaty of Birgham, it is hardly surprising that a clash occurred early in John Balliol's kingship. On 8 May 1293, John was summoned before the King's Bench to answer for his failure to do justice in the case of John Mazun, a Bordeaux wine merchant who was owed money by Alexander III. When Mazun died, and the lawsuit became void, another appeal – from Macduff of Fife who complained to Edward I that he had not received justice in King John's court concerning his inheritance of lands – was scheduled for 24 May. Although he had rehearsed his answers and been coached by his more experienced counsellors, John Balliol was inexperienced in such matters. The King was put under severe pressure by Edward I, who judged him to be in his mercy for contempt of court and threatened him with the forfeiture of his three chief castles and towns (probably Edinburgh, Roxburgh and Berwick). Under the circumstances Balliol abandoned all resistance and once more acknowledged Edward's overlordship in abject terms.

A year afterwards, following the outbreak of war between England and France, in June 1294, Edward I summoned John Balliol, ten Scottish earls and sixteen barons to perform personal feudal service against the French. Not since 1159 had a King of Scotland performed overseas military service for a King of England. Again John Balliol seemed weak on this issue as a month earlier he appeared to offer aid to Edward I. When the summons came, on 29 June 1294, Balliol, undoubtedly under pressure from his baronial advisers, made excuses. As the Welsh rose in revolt in September 1294, which was due partly to Edward's demand for them to fight for him against the French, Scottish prevarication on their summons could not be dealt with immediately. Indeed, the fact that the Welsh rebellion lasted until March 1295 may have encouraged Scottish leaders to assert independent action. By December 1294, they had absolution from the Pope freeing them from any oaths exacted from them under duress. The Scottish political community also sought help from the French in order to preserve the independence of the Scottish kingdom. Discussions had taken place between March and May, and by 5 July 1295, King John addressed letters to Philip IV appointing four persons to negotiate in

The Great Seal of John Balliol, King of the Scots, which is dated 21 November 1295. Obverse: the King, for whom William Wallace fought, is seated on a throne, with curling hair and large crown with three fleurs-de-lis, in loose girdled robe and cloak, the cords of which he holds with his left hand while in his right he holds a sceptre with large foliated top. The throne has a back of openwork with two high and two low crocheted finials, also a footboard on a corbel. At each side of the throne is a shield bearing arms – an orb (Balliol) and a lion rampant (Galloway – Balliol was Lord of Galloway). (By permission of the Court of the Lord Lyon.)

France regarding John Balliol's son, Edward, and a relative of Philip. At the same July Parliament, in another key move, government was taken out of the hands of John Balliol and given to a Council of Twelve who would assume control on behalf of King John. The treaty with France followed on 23 October 1295, and was ratified by the Scottish King and Parliament on 23 February 1296.

The treaty with France amounted, in practice, to a Scottish declaration of war against the English. In fact a summons to the host went out to assemble on 22 March. It is important to understand the stance taken by James Stewart and his following within the Scottish political community on the eve of the Scottish wars. The Stewarts were regarded as indispensable parts of Scottish government under John Balliol's kingship because of their power and landed influence in the west. Their role had been consolidated from the days of Alexander III and the Guardians. However, the Stewarts, in the person of James Stewart, were still not part of the inner core of central Scottish government and did not take a leading role in the negotiations for the Franco-Scottish treaty. Yet Stewart supported government actions and the stand against English interference, and he was one of the Council of Twelve chosen to direct Scottish

Coldstream, looking towards England. Edward I invaded Scotland in 1296, crossing the Tweed near this point, and then moved in the direction of Berwick.

government on behalf of John Balliol. In 1295, James Stewart was given added responsibility for the important border castle of Roxburgh. As a member of the Council of Twelve (together with his ally, Robert Wishart, Bishop of Glasgow), he undoubtedly adhered to the policy of the Scottish government if not necessarily to the Comyn-dominated leadership of that body. No doubt, Stewart and Wishart supported the words of defiance by which John Balliol (or the government acting on his behalf) formally renounced his homage to Edward I on 5 April 1296:

> You yourself and others of your realm . . . have caused harm beyond measure to the liberties of ourselves and of our kingdom . . . for instance by summoning us outside our realm at the mere beck and call of anybody, as your whim dictated, and by harassing us unjustifiably . . . now you have come to the frontiers of our realm in warlike array, with a vast concourse of soldiers . . . to disinherit us and the inhabitants of our realm . . . we desire to assert ourselves against you, for our own defence and that of our realm, to whose defence and safekeeping we are constrained by the bond of an oath and so by

Berwick Castle. On 30 March 1296 the town of Berwick, then only surrounded by a ditch and timber palisade for defence, was attacked by the English army of Edward I and many people killed. Edward strengthened the town walls and Berwick became the focal point for his direct rule over Scotland after the Battle of Dunbar.

the present letter we renounce the fealty and homage which we have done to you . . .

The Stewarts, and presumably their followers such as the Wallaces, were committed to war against Edward I in order to preserve their position of power in Scotland. They tied their fortunes, as did the Comyns and their associates in government, to the principles of an independent Scotland, which had been upheld by the ruling aristocracy in Scotland since the second half of the thirteenth century. It is interesting, however, that the Bruces, close family allies of the Stewarts but excluded from Scottish government, did not respond to the Scottish host – in fact, Robert Bruce the elder, the leader of the Bruces after the death of his father in 1295, and his son (the future King) testified on 25 March that they had already done homage to Edward. In the Scottish wars, the Bruces started on the English side with Robert Bruce, the elder, defending Carlisle Castle for Edward I. His son forfeited the earldom of Carrick. The Bruces were not the only noble families to swear to support Edward I: Patrick, Earl of Dunbar, and Gilbert Umphraville, Earl of Angus, also sided with Edward I when war with the Scottish government seemed probable.

Hostilities broke out on 26 March 1296 with an attack on Bruce-controlled Carlisle by John Comyn, Earl of Buchan, six other earls of

Spott Burn. It was near here, in the vicinity of Dunbar, that the Scottish army suffered a major defeat at the hands of the English army on 27 April 1296 at the very beginning of the Scottish wars.

Scotland and John Comyn, the younger. James Stewart was once again not involved in front-line activities, though whether he would actually have wished to participate in an assault on family allies, the Bruces, is questionable. At about the same time, the English army was gathering around Berwick and on 30 March the town was stormed and many townsmen (by one exaggerated account, over 11,000) were butchered. In reprisal, another Scottish raiding party, based at Jedburgh (which had been under Comyn control in the early 1290s) attacked Northumberland, particularly Redesdale, Coquetdale and Tynedale. On their way back from this action they took Dunbar with the help of the Comyn Countess of Dunbar who, unlike her husband, remained loyal to the Scottish government. It was at Dunbar on 27 April that the first phase of the Scottish wars took a decisive turn when the Scottish army, trying to relieve the siege of the town by English troops, was routed and those within the castle surrendered.

Dunbar was a conclusive defeat for Scotland, though the scale of Scottish casualties – estimated at 10,000 dead by the Lanercost chronicler – is probably greatly exaggerated. Certainly only one major Scottish aristocrat, Patrick Graham, is known to have been killed and it seems that most nobles soon abandoned the conflict. It is probable that the full Scottish host were not present and that neither John Balliol nor James Stewart was involved in the battle. Indeed, James Stewart surrendered Roxburgh Castle to the English only a week after Dunbar and on 13 May swore fealty to King Edward. It seems that Stewart was seeking to distance himself from the Comyns and their allies who had clearly lost their political control over Scotland at Dunbar. By so doing, Stewart hoped to maintain his position of authority in western Scotland. His policy seemed to work for he was soon being employed by Edward I to receive the surrender of two castles within his area of influence, Kirkintilloch and Dumbarton. A marriage alliance between James Stewart and Egidia, sister of Richard Burgh, Earl of Ulster and one of Edward I's close supporters, was, no doubt, intended to consolidate Stewart's loyalty. According to John of Fordun, the elder Robert Bruce also approached Edward I with hope of reward for the Bruce family in Scotland, only to be rebuffed unceremoniously, 'Have we nothing else to do but win kingdoms for thee?' Even the Comyns, whose leading members had fled along with John Balliol to the Comyn-dominated north of Scotland, adopted a more pragmatic policy, returning south to seek favourable surrender terms from the English King.

Edward I had tried to control the Comyns and, through them, the Scottish King, who was a puppet of his relatives, the Comyns, rather than Edward I. He had shown favour to the family and their allies in Scotland when he was overlord in 1291 and 1292, and also in England. By 1293, John Comyn, heir of the senior Badenoch branch of the Comyn family,

Dunbar Castle and harbour. Few medieval remains of the castle exist today, it having been ruined by Order of Parliament in 1567. William Wallace does not seem to have been present at the Battle of Dunbar, 1296, but he certainly emerged, with William Douglas among others, in the aftermath of this severe Scottish defeat and the beginning of English direct rule.

was married to Joan Valence, daughter of William, Earl of Pembroke, and cousin of the English King. By a mixture of favour and threat – Edward I made it clear to the Comyns and Balliol how much they were under his financial control – the English King hoped to use Comyn power and influence across Scotland to secure political stability as well as his own interests.

The events of 1295 and 1296 proved Edward I wrong. It also showed that he could not ride roughshod over the strong feelings of national independence held by the Scottish government without provoking a reaction. Unfortunately, Edward I did not learn this lesson immediately, partly because of the deceptive ease with which Scotland had been conquered in 1296. After key Scottish castles such as Roxburgh, Edinburgh and Stirling had surrendered soon after Dunbar, Edward I marched north through Scotland via Perth, Montrose, Banff and Elgin to impose his authority. On 8 July 1296, at Montrose, King John Balliol formally submitted to Edward, resigning his kingdom to the English King and having his coat of royal arms stripped from his tabard in a public and humiliating manner. In July and August, Edward I visited royal centres

Banff, an important royal centre in northern Scotland by the late twelfth century. However, it was removed from English possession by Andrew Moray during the successful summer of Scottish resistance in 1297.

such as Aberdeen, Banff and Elgin, which had been under Comyn influence, and sent commissioners to search more remote areas in the north such as the district of Badenoch, the lordship of the senior Comyn branch. Edward also took the homages of the leading men of Scotland during his progress through Scotland. This was followed by the swearing of fealty to Edward by every freeholder.

At first, after Dunbar, Edward I did seem willing to negotiate with those who exercised power and influence in Scotland. Initially, even with John Balliol, he was prepared to discuss terms. Apparently Anthony Bek and John Warenne, Earl of Surrey (Balliol had married Isabel, second daughter of Warenne in 1281), were sent with a compromise proposal – Balliol would receive an English earldom; in return Edward would be granted Scotland. Similarly, initially Edward accepted James Stewart's early surrender in return for using him as one of his agents in Scotland. The Bruces also seemed to expect Edward I to bring them into power in Scotland. However, the expectations of both Bruces and Stewarts were soon to be dashed as Edward decided, instead of employing them in Scotland, to take charge himself. This significant toughening of stance undoubtedly influenced the roles of James Stewart and the younger Robert Bruce (the future King) in the 1297 revolt.

Edward I's assumption of direct control of Scottish government was seen in a number of his actions. His takeover was demonstrated most clearly by his removal of the Stone of Destiny, the most precious symbol of Scottish monarchy, from Scone Abbey to Westminster Abbey. Other Scottish muniments and government records were seized. This was a direct contravention of the rights of the Scots agreed in the Treaty of Birgham in 1290, 'the relics, charters, privileges and other muniments which concern the royal dignity and realm of Scotland shall be deposited in a secure place within the realm of Scotland'. Though Edward I no longer regarded the terms of the treaty as valid, the leaders of the Scottish political community definitely did. The removal of the Scottish King and the mainstays of Scottish government, the Comyns and their allies, to England was part of the same English policy. It should be noted that Edward I's twenty-one-week search through Scotland was concentrated in areas that were under the influence of the Comyn family and their allies in northern Scotland. No fewer than eight members of the Comyn family were committed to detention in England. Other powerful families in Scottish government were also imprisoned in England – members of the Moray family, including Andrew Moray who was Justiciar of Scotia, members of the Mowbray, Balliol, Macdougall, Graham and Randolph families who had been mainstays of government, similarly members of the Sinclair, Lochore, Cheyne, Ros and de la Hay families who held a number of sheriffdoms. Edward I hoped to teach the Comyns and their supporters, involved in both central and local government, a harsh lesson.

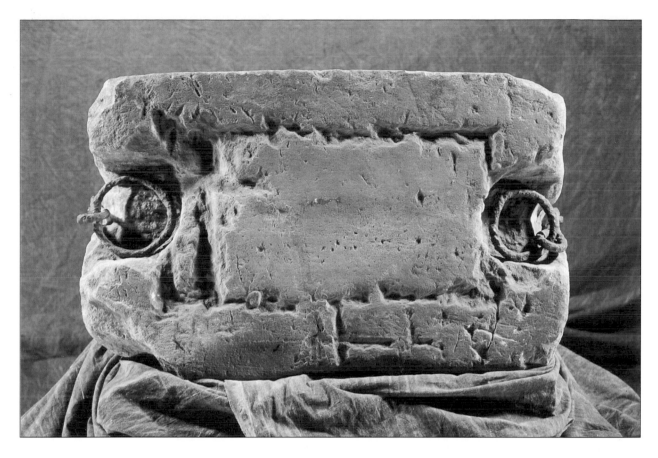

The Stewarts tried to dissociate themselves from the Comyns and win English favour by an early submission to Edward I after Dunbar. The Bruces hoped they would be asked by Edward to start a Bruce dynasty and an alternative Scottish government, friendly to the English King. However, there was disappointment for both parties as Edward I refused to fill the political vacuum he had created. Instead, Edward gave responsibilities to his own officials, John Warenne, Earl of Surrey, as Lieutenant Keeper of Scotland, Hugh Cressingham as Treasurer and Walter Amersham as Chancellor. The headquarters for Edward I's new government in Scotland was established at Berwick and the English pattern of administration was adopted with two escheators for north and south of the Forth. Edward hoped to achieve stability within Scotland by restoring lands to those who swore fealty to him and had not been involved in the war against him.

Thus far, there is no mention in historical record of William Wallace or his family and the motivations of that family can only be guessed at in the context of their lords, the Stewarts. The background factors to take into consideration in understanding William Wallace's emergence onto the military and political stage are: the development of an increasingly mature Scottish government by the end of the thirteenth century with a clear sense of identity and a keen desire for independence; the interplay

The top of the Stone of Destiny. This most precious symbol of Scottish monarchy and Scottish nationhood was removed from Scone Abbey to Westminster Abbey as a demonstration of Edward I's policy of direct rule following his victory at Dunbar in April 1296. (Crown Copyright: Reproduced courtesy of Historic Scotland.)

The Stone of Destiny with the Honours of Scotland. The Stone of Destiny, symbol of what William Wallace was fighting for, was returned from Westminster to Scotland in November 1996. It is now kept with the Honours of Scotland in Edinburgh Castle. (Crown Copyright: Reproduced courtesy of Historic Scotland.)

between different aristocratic power groups both within government (the dominant Comyns and their associates, and the non-Comyn grouping including the Stewarts) and outside it (chiefly the Bruces); the increasingly interventionist policy of Edward I since 1289; and finally the implementation of Edward's policy of direct rule in Scotland after the submission of John Balliol in July 1296 and the political exile in England of the Scottish families of government that followed.

It has been seen that the Stewarts were a part of the aristocratic governing community that clearly articulated a policy of national independence in the difficult years after Alexander III's death in 1286. They were not, however, allies of the Comyns and their associates who dominated most of the key government positions at the centre as well as in the localities. Indeed, the Stewarts had family sympathies with the Bruces and supported their claims to the Scottish kingship during the 'Great Cause' of 1291–2. The Stewarts supported war with England, although the exact nature of their involvement in the war efforts of 1296 is unclear. They did not, like their family allies the Bruces, side with

Edward I before the outbreak of hostilities. The Stewarts were independent-minded enough within Scotland to make an early submission after English victory at Dunbar in the hope of preserving their power and influence in western Scotland under a new Scottish regime more greatly influenced by Edward I. As far as the Stewarts' followers were concerned, it would seem natural, after James Stewart's early swearing of fealty on 13 May 1296 and his brother John's on 15 May, for them to do the same. That this happened is attested by Edward I's employment of Stewart and his henchmen in receiving the surrender of the castles of Kirkintilloch and Dumbarton (the latter, of course, had formerly been in Stewart's hands as Sheriff of Dumbarton) on about 10 June.

A list of Stewart followers in the 'Ragman Roll' under the date of 28 August is impressively wide-ranging. There are a number of important absences, however. William Wallace is not mentioned, and even if he was in 1296 of insufficient age or status to be named, it is certainly odd that his elder brother, Malcolm, is not referred to. The Wallace name does, however, feature on the list – Alan Wallace, Adam le Wallace, John la Wallace Fitz Thomas le Wallace, Nicol le Wallace and John la Wallace of Over Etone. Evidence from William Wallace's seal of 1297 suggests that this Alan Wallace may have been William Wallace's father. All those who submitted to Edward I had their lands restored to them. As for the Stewarts' tenants and sub-tenants, on 8 September the Sheriffs of Ayr and Lanark as well as those of Berwick, Edinburgh and Roxburgh were commanded to return the lands that had been confiscated. The evidence from the 'Ragman Roll' suggests that the Wallaces – if not William, his elder brother (or brothers) – had had their lands seized and did not recover them. They would have had the status of outlaws. William Wallace's sense of family grievance would have been exacerbated if, as suggested by both Andrew Wyntoun and Blind Harry, William's father and/or an elder brother had been slain by the English. The legal record of 8 August 1296 that refers to a 'William le Waleys, thief' in Perth could tie in with William Wallace as a man on the run, though this may be stretching probability. A sense of injustice regarding land rather than the traditional tale referring to the capture and murder of his supposed mistress, Marion Braidfute, who is described as his wife by Blind Harry, seems to provide a more likely motivation for turning against the Sheriff of Lanark in 1297. It also seems probable, based on John of Fordun's evidence, that William Wallace was already an outlaw before his attack on the Sheriff of Lanark.

In terms of the debate about William Wallace being an individual adventurer or merely an agent of his overlord, the Stewarts, the evidence suggests that initially, at least, Wallace was operating on his own. Wallace and his elder brother, Malcolm, did not swear fealty to Edward I in 1296. Perhaps their father's homage was deemed sufficient. James Stewart's decision to seek alliance with Edward I in May 1296 may have been caused by Edward's attempt to extend English influence in western Scotland in April 1296. In this month, he appointed Alexander Macdonald of Islay as Baillie of Kintyre, an area formerly under James Stewart's jurisdiction. Edward I's employment of Stewart and his supporters in June 1296 and the marriage of James Stewart into the Burgh family, close followers of the King, suggested that the Stewarts would retain their influence in western Scotland with the King's support. However, Edward I's policy towards Scotland itself, i.e. direct rule, and therefore his attitude towards the Stewarts, changed during the summer of 1296. Edward I nominated Henry Percy as English Warden of Ayr and Galloway in September 1296. This was a real blow to Stewart power and control in the region, especially after his loss of power in Kintyre earlier in the year. By September 1296, rather later than William Wallace, the Stewarts had developed a strong motivation for revolt.

Concentration on the role of William Wallace and the Stewarts in the rebellion of 1297 has tended to distract attention from unrest in other parts of Scotland than the south-west. Indeed, it is probable that the revolt in northern Scotland involving the Moray and Macdougall families preceded the activities of William Wallace in the south. To understand why there was insurrection in both northern and southern Scotland in 1297, who spearheaded these uprisings and who supported them, it is necessary to look a little more closely at the activities of Edward I's English administration in Scotland in 1296 and 1297.

Recent research by Fiona Watson in *Under the Hammer: Edward I and Scotland 1286–1306* (East Linton, Tuckwell Press, 1998) has shed more light on the English impact on Scotland and therefore the possible causes of resentment that contributed to the revolts of 1297. It is apparent that Edward I concentrated most of his resources south of the Forth, no doubt to consolidate English authority from his new centre of administration in Scotland, Berwick. In the north, there is little evidence of how he sought to impose English authority. Presumably he thought that Scotland north of the Forth would be suitably impressed (perhaps cowed) by his royal progress around the main royal castles, burghs and baronial centres there. Following this, English garrisons appear to have been placed at Aberdeen (under Henry Lathum) and at Urquhart (under William Fitz Warin). In the north, Edward seems to have used a mixture of English officials and Scots, apparently intimidated into acting on Edward's behalf by the imprisonment of family members in England. In the latter category was Reginald Cheyne, senior, who was Sheriff of Inverness, Euphemia, the Countess of Ross, and Gartnait, son and heir of Donald, Earl of Mar. In addition, an Englishman, Henry Rye, was appointed escheator north of the Forth with custody of the royal castles of Elgin and Forres. Following Scottish administrative practice, another official, a justiciar of Scotland north of the Forth, was appointed – once again an Englishman, William Mortimer.

Rather more evidence exists for a more thoroughly English administrative system south of the Forth. As well as Edward's triumvirate of chief officials – John Warenne, Earl of Surrey (Lieutenant), Walter Amersham (Chancellor) and Hugh Cressingham (Treasurer) – that was based in southern Scotland, there was a Justiciar of Lothian (William of Ormesby) and a Justiciar of Galloway (Roger Skoter), an escheator south of the Forth (Peter Dunwich) and, after 8 September 1296, the Warden of Ayr and Galloway (Henry Percy). In addition, most of the new sheriffs in Scotland after 1296 would have lacked any connection with the local community or, indeed, Scotland in general and were probably unable to speak the local language. In the south-west of Scotland, for instance, it is unlikely that the new officials could communicate in Gaelic, as the Stewarts, Bruces and Wallaces probably could, and this would have reinforced the feeling that the area had been taken over in a hostile manner.

What was the impact of these English office-holders on Scottish communities? Certainly the attitudes of some of the more senior people

Castle Urquhart. Situated on Strone Point on the western shore of Loch Ness, Urquhart controlled the strategic route along the Great Glen to Inverness. It was, therefore, a terrific boost to Scottish resistance when Andrew Moray recaptured this English-held castle in 1297.

must have caused resentment. Even the English chronicler, Walter of Guisborough, referred to Hugh Cressingham as 'a self-important and proud man who loved money'. The collection of funds from the native population had been a feature of Edward's policy in Ireland and Wales and the apparent lack of Scottish military resistance to English forces in 1296 may well have given Edward and his officials the impression that there would be relatively little resistance to financial exactions. Initially, a large sum, over £5,000, was raised and Walter of Guisborough's description of Cressingham as a man 'who robbed too much' seemed justifiable. The fact that by late July 1297, this flow of money had practically stopped is surely a sign of general Scottish resistance to these demands. Cressingham wrote to Edward in late July that 'no county is in proper order excepting Berwick and Roxburgh', and slightly later,

> . . . from the time when I left you, not a penny could be raised in your realm by any means until my lord the earl of Warenne shall enter your land and compel the people of your country by force and sentences of law . . .

According to the *Guisborough Chronicle*, persecution of those who did not swear fealty to Edward I was a particular fault of the Justiciar William Ormesby and another cause of resentment. The threat of military service overseas, on the part of 'all the middle people of Scotland', was a concern expressed during the surrender negotiations after one of the revolts in the south-west was halted. Such a fear would have affected most classes from the nobles, who might have to supply personal knight service, to the non-noble foot soldiers, who had sometimes been conscripted for campaigns from Ireland and especially Wales as well as from the English counties. There is no real proof that this was what Edward I intended, though there is evidence that fifty-seven Scottish nobles were summoned on 24 May 1297 to serve Edward I in Flanders. In addition, the compulsory seizure of wool, one of the chief economic assets of Scotland, must have been another source of both indignation and apprehension (of where the next appropriation or enforced sale would be). It is known that such confiscations took place at both Melrose Abbey and Sweetheart Abbey.

There has been a natural tendency to focus on what the Scots were fighting against in 1297 rather than what they were fighting for and to give more attention to revolt in the south than the north. Yet rebellion in Scotland in 1297 probably started earlier in the north and involved two families who had something to fight for as well as against. The Macdougalls and the Morays had been stalwarts of Scottish government and in 1296 that regime's figurehead was John Balliol. Both Macdougalls and Morays were related to the Comyns, the power behind the Scottish King (who was, of course, also related to the Comyns). Macdougalls and Morays had enjoyed the power that went with holding public office and it was unlikely that they would willingly consent to losing this. Macdougall control in the north-west was seriously threatened by Edward I's appointment of Alexander Macdonald of Islay in April 1296 as Baillie in the sheriffdoms of Lorn, Ross and the Isles. Edward I presumably thought that with Alexander Macdougall of Argyll having done homage to him and being a prisoner in Berwick Castle the rest of the Macdougall family would cause him no problems. However, Alexander's son, Duncan, who had never sworn loyalty to Edward I, led the Macdougall resistance to Macdonald's attempt to control 'their' area using the strategic castle of their Comyn allies at Inverlochy to aid their fight.

The Seal of John Moray, c. 1250. From the mid-thirteenth century the Morays were an increasingly prominent family in government. It is against this background that Andrew Moray's role should be judged. (By permission of the Court of the Lord Lyon.)

Even more important in the insurrections of 1297, however, were the Morays, another of Scotland's 'government' families. A successful revolt in northern Scotland was led by Andrew Moray, son of Andrew Moray of Petty who had been Justiciar of Scotia during the Balliol kingship (to 1296) and deemed important enough to be imprisoned in the Tower of London. The younger Andrew had himself been imprisoned at Chester but had escaped to lead an impressively effective campaign against English bases across northern Scotland. The efforts of both Morays and Macdougalls in 1297 could both be seen as motivated by patriotism and self-interest. They were representatives of John Balliol's government and were seeking to defend their privileged positions within it. They also symbolised a resistance to Edward I's infringements of the rights of the kingdom and a defence of the principles encapsulated in the Treaty of Birgham (1290), 'the rights, laws, liberties and customs of the same realms of Scotland to be preserved in every respect and in all time coming throughout the said realm and its borders completely and without being impaired . . .'. Such ideas epitomised the feelings of those families involved in the governing of Scotland in 1296 and the views of the same families who were able, in 1297, to translate theory into military action.

The young Andrew Moray soon recaptured the English held castles in the north, including Inverness, Urquhart, Banff, Elgin and Aberdeen between May and mid-July 1297. This area had been very much under

Elgin Cathedral. Andrew Moray recaptured a series of English-held castles in northern Scotland during the summer of 1297. These included Urquhart, Banff, Elgin and Aberdeen. Elgin Cathedral, regarded as one of the most beautiful Scottish cathedrals, was founded in 1224 as the seat of the bishopric of Moray. Much of the structure dates from the thirteenth century.

Comyn influence and it is worth noting the family relationship by marriage between the Morays and the Comyns. Both Morays and Macdougalls were part of the Comyn patronage system. Evidence from letters to Edward I from northern Scotland indicate that Andrew Moray soon acquired popular support in the region. He had 'a very large body of rogues' and this army of foot soldiers fought 'guerrilla-type' warfare as 'they betook themselves into a very great strong-hold of bog and wood, where no horsemen could be of service'.

Rather more attention has been paid to the rebellion in the south of Scotland, which involved two apparently separate risings. One was led by James Stewart, Bishop Wishart and Robert Bruce, and is generally seen as an aristocratic revolt, and the other was organised by William Wallace, and is usually viewed as a 'spontaneous act of middling and common folk'(A.A.M. Duncan, 'The Community of the Realm of Scotland and Robert Bruce', *Scottish Historical Review* XLV [1966]). Too much contrast has been made between the 'official' revolt of Bishop Wishart and James Stewart (who were joined by the young Robert Bruce) and the 'popular' revolt of William Wallace. The Lanercost chronicler thought that the rising was planned and instigated by Wishart and Stewart who

> . . . caused a certain bloody man, William Wallace, who had formerly been a chief of brigands in Scotland to revolt against the king and assemble the people in revolt . . .

It seems, however, that Wallace's rebellion had already started by early May at the latest. The active involvement of Wishart and Stewart may have been provoked by Edward I's demand for over fifty Scottish nobles to give military service overseas in his campaign in Flanders. This summons was issued on 24 May and it is unlikely that they came out in open revolt before then.

William Wallace's first action on historical record, as has been mentioned, was the assault and murder of the English Sheriff of Lanark, William Heselrigg. The Sheriff was apparently at Lanark holding a local court at the time of the attack. Most information about the incident comes from the fourteenth-century *Scalacronica* of Thomas Gray, whose father was an eyewitness to events.

> The said William Wallace came by night upon the said sheriff and surprised him, when Thomas de Gray [father of the chronicler] who was at that time in the suite of the said sheriff, was left stripped for dead in the mellay when the English were defending themselves. The said Thomas lay all night naked between two burning houses which the Scots had set on fire, whereof the heat kept life in him, until he

Monkton church, Ayrshire. This is where a priest, according to Blind Harry's narrative, interpreted a dream that Wallace had had – Wallace received confirmation that he should fight for Scotland and that he had Church support.

was recognised at daybreak and carried off by William of Lundy, who caused him to be restored to health.

It is probable that this attack was motivated by something personal to Wallace and that he was already an outlaw by this time. As Sheriff, Heselrigg had responsibility for the organisation of fealty-taking to Edward I as well as property matters in his area and it may have been, as argued in Chapter 2, that Wallace's grievance was a family one relating to swearing fealty and/or the confiscation of property. As the Guisborough chronicler points out, there was persecution by some English officials of those who did not wish to pledge their allegiance to the King of England. While in the *Lanercost Chronicle* William Wallace is referred to as a 'certain bloody man . . . who had formerly been chief of brigands in Scotland', Walter of Guisborough's earliest reference to Wallace is as 'a vagrant fugitive' who 'called all the exiles to himself and made himself almost their prince: they grew to be numerous'. Thus, at first, it seems that William Wallace was an independent adventurer, motivated by the persecution of his family by the English.

Clearly, however, William Wallace was not the only one with a complaint against the English. An early associate of Wallace's, according to Walter of Guisborough, was William Douglas who had been in command of Berwick Castle in 1296 and had to surrender it to the English. Douglas had a reputation as a troublemaker to both the Guardians and Edward I. He was known to Edward I for his rash actions in abducting and marrying by force an English widow, Eleanor Ferrers, who was staying with relatives in Scotland. However, after his surrender at Berwick:

When the king had restored everything to him he became unmindful of these good deeds and turned robber working with a robber . . . the two Williams with perverse people thought they could find the justiciar of the king at Scone, where he had heard pleas, and they hastened to destroy him. But he was forewarned and escaped with difficulty, leaving to the enemy many spoils.

It is unlikely that the attack on the Justiciar William Ormesby was a random attack. It is Walter of Guisborough again who notes that Ormesby was a particularly intense prosecutor of 'all those who did not wish to swear fealty to the king of England without making distinction of person'. The Douglas family were related to the Stewarts by marriage and also to the Morays. William Douglas, before his infamous abduction of Eleanor Ferrers, was married to James Stewart's sister, Elizabeth. This common association with the Stewarts gives further backing to the assertion by the Lanercost and Guisborough chroniclers that James Stewart was one of the 'authors of the whole evil' (*Guisborough Chronicle*).

Scone Cross. Scone played a prominent part in the early years of the Scottish wars. It was important symbolically as the King of Scots was traditionally crowned at Scone Abbey where the Stone of Destiny was kept. Thus the raid of William Wallace and William Douglas on William Ormesby, the Justiciar and therefore one of Edward I's most important officials, while he was holding court there, was a very significant development.

Overleaf: Loudoun Hill. This area was, in fact, the location of a skirmish fought by Robert Bruce in June 1307. Blind Harry transferred the episode to William Wallace's career and made it the place where Wallace gained revenge for the death of his father

It seems that Stewart secretly backed the risings of Wallace and Douglas before coming out openly against Edward I in about July 1297. According to Walter of Guisborough, Wallace, while at Perth, received messengers 'in great haste on behalf of certain magnates of the kingdom of Scotland', probably Stewart and Wishart. In this escalation of his resistance, Stewart was joined in alliance again with Bishop Robert Wishart of Glasgow, who had a distinguished record of outspoken opposition to Edward I's interventionist approach. The involvement of Stewart and Bishop Wishart, who had acted as Guardians and had played active roles in the government of John Balliol, certainly gave their military endeavours an 'official' character. Contemporary chroniclers, as well as later historians, have tended to pay more attention to this revolt because of two of the participants' seniority within the Scottish ruling hierarchy. As has been seen, Stewart had been threatened in his attempt to stay in public office and retain political power in western Scotland under Edward I. Now, Stewart and Wishart, it is clear from the negotiation terms following their ignominious surrender at Irvine in early July 1297, regarded themselves as leaders and representatives of the 'whole community of the realm of Scotland' (from the Treaty at Irvine) and John Balliol's kingship.

An interesting twist to this so-called 'aristocratic revolt' – Andrew Moray and William Douglas were also noblemen – was the involvement of the young Robert Bruce, Earl of Carrick, and future King, as one of the leaders alongside Stewart and Wishart. Robert Bruce had been exiled with his father by the Comyn/Balliol government – his father had not sworn fealty to Balliol and they had both been on Edward's side at the outbreak of war in 1296. The fact that Edward I showed no inclination to reward the Bruces after Dunbar with either the kingship of Scotland or even political power in Scotland may have persuaded the younger Bruce to join in the 1297 revolt after it had started. The Guisborough chronicler believes that Bruce was already aiming at the throne. It seems more probable, however, that he was, as a first step, trying to use his military power as a Scottish earl and his family friendship with the Stewarts and Wisharts to establish himself as one of the chief leaders of the Scottish political community in the absence of his Scottish rivals, the Comyns and John Balliol.

Despite the ease of the English victory over Wishart, Stewart and Bruce at Irvine, rebellion in Scotland was beginning to trouble Edward I. The surrender negotiations lasted for some time and it may have been that there was a deliberate attempt by the three leaders to procrastinate and draw attention away from revolts elsewhere in Scotland. Meanwhile, Edward I who was generally, in 1297, more concerned with his expedition to Flanders, sought to use the Comyns and their associates in government in late June 1297 (duly chastened, he hoped, by their defeat, political exile and imprisonment in England in 1296–7)

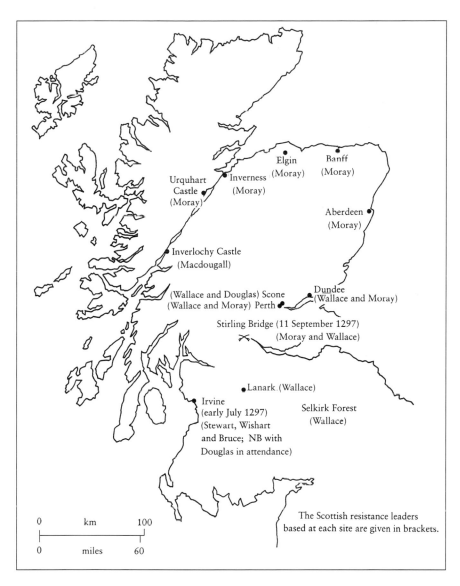

The Scottish resistance leaders based at each site are given in brackets.

Scottish resistance in 1297 before the Battle of Stirling Bridge, 11 September 1297.

to restore order in Scotland. The role of the Comyns was vital given their dominance over central and local government in Scotland prior to 1296. In the north, John Comyn, Earl of Buchan, and his brother, Alexander, were sent to help Henry Cheyne, Bishop of Aberdeen, the Countess of Ross and Gartnait, son of the Earl of Mar, to control the rebellion of Andrew Moray. John Comyn of Badenoch was commanded by Edward I to assist Brian Fitz Alan, the new custodian of the kingdom, in the south. Alexander Macdougall had been released from prison at Berwick on 24 May 1297, a month earlier than the Comyns, to help dissuade his son from continuing his revolt in the north-west. The news from Hugh Cressingham in late July and early August 1297 cast doubt on either the ability or the willingness of the Comyns to promote Edward I's interests in Scotland (in a letter of 5 August 1297 to Edward I):

Ettrick Forest, above Moffatt, the base for William Wallace's military efforts both before and after the Battle of Stirling Bridge. In areas such as these, the historical William Wallace and the 'Scottish Robin Hood' tradition of the fifteenth century come more closely together.

. . . in some counties the Scotch have established and placed bailiffs and ministers so that no county is in proper order excepting Berwick and Roxburgh . . . the peace on the other side of the Scottish sea is still in obscurity, as it is said, as to the doings of the earls [the Comyns are meant here] who are there . . .

According to the *Guisborough Chronicle*, John Comyn, Earl of Buchan, 'at first pretended to repress rebellion, but in the end changed sides and became a thorn in our flesh'. The Comyns did not come out openly in support of revolt and resume their leadership role within Scotland – the presence of John Comyn, the younger, of Badenoch, heir of the senior branch of the family, in Edward I's army in Flanders may have dissuaded the Comyns from an open stance. However, the ability of the Scots to establish their own officers and the ability of Moray to gather a large infantry unit in the Comyn-dominated north and make his way to join Wallace's forces in the south strongly suggests collusion with the Comyns. Moray and his forces had military control as far south as Perth and were preparing to meet up with Wallace's troops. Meanwhile, Wallace took advantage of the delays after the Irvine capitulation to gather a large company in the forest of Selkirk 'like one who holds himself against your peace' (letter from Hugh Cressingham to Edward I, 23 July 1297).

In the context of lackadaisical English command in Scotland and, it seems, wide-scale sabotage of the English administration in the country, Wallace's following grew in number and strength. According to the *Guisborough Chronicle*:

> . . . that bandit Wallace gathered the people to him . . . By now, indeed, he had raised an immense army, for all the common folk of the land followed him as their general and prince. All the retainers and tenants of the nobleman also came in to him, and though the nobles themselves were with our king in body, yet their hearts had long been with their own people . . .

Wallace's forces, having replenished and equipped themselves at Bishop Wishart's manor at Ancrum, moved north from Selkirk Forest to meet Andrew Moray's unit near Perth. The combined strength of Wallace and Moray was great enough to besiege Dundee.

In early September, however, the delayed English reaction at last happened – as late as 26 September 1297, the English still believed that John Comyn, Earl of Buchan, remained loyal. Revolt in Scotland had escalated and sparked off an increasingly violent general rising between Forth and

Howe of Mearns. It is known that William Wallace and William Douglas were at Scone, but Blind Harry's narrative has Wallace proceeding afterwards north through the Mearns.

Dunnotar Castle. There is no historical record of Wallace laying siege to any castle north of Dundee, though Blind Harry's account has Wallace – it was, more probably, Andrew Moray – besieging and capturing Dunnotar Castle. This castle, taken by Edward I in 1296, has spectacular natural defences. No part of the present structure is earlier than the late fourteenth-century keep.

Strathfillan. Blind Harry's description of Wallace's campaigns north of Glasgow through Strathfillan to Loch Dochart is rather reminiscent of Robert Bruce's campaigns in this area in 1307.

Loch Etive. Blind Harry says that Wallace spent some time on the north shore of this loch.

Tay, backed in this area by Macduff, son of the Earl of Fife. News of the increasingly racial attacks on the English in Scotland, including clerics, were related to the monks at Guisborough, apparently by an eyewitness:

> They even dragged English monks violently from monasteries . . . and made a sport and spectacle of them . . . Among their victims were two English canons of St. Andrews, who were carried to the

bridge at Perth . . . they stood there, being subjected to a kind of mock-trial before that bandit Wallace and expecting death at any moment . . . three Englishmen who had been given a house at St. Andrews . . . fled from Wallace and his men and ran to the sacred stone called St. Andrew's Needle, believing that they would be protected by the sanctuary of Holy Church: but the Scots pursued them, and cut them down at that very stone . . .

Such incidents were, perhaps, necessary to provoke a reaction from the slothful, indecisive English commanders in Scotland.

Ardchattan Priory, on the north side of Loch Etive. According to Blind Harry, Wallace held a council here but there is no historical evidence for this. It may be another example of the poet taking episodes from Robert Bruce's campaigns and adding them to Wallace's record.

4

GUERRILLA TO GOVERNOR

The period between May 1297 and March 1298 saw William Wallace rise in meteoric fashion to military and political leadership in Scotland. Although it is fairly certain that he was an outlaw when he murdered William Heselrigg, the English Sheriff of Lanark, in the early summer of 1297, within a few months Wallace was being viewed in an entirely different way. By 11 October 1297 – after victory over the English at the Battle of Stirling Bridge (11 September) – Wallace was describing himself, together with Andrew Moray, as joint leader at Stirling Bridge, as 'leaders of the army of the kingdom of Scotland' (letter to the towns of Lübeck and Hamburg). On 29 March 1298 Wallace defined himself in another official document, the Charter of William Wallace to Alexander Scrymgeour, as

> . . . knight, Guardian of the kingdom of Scotland and commander of its army, in the name of the famous prince the lord John, by God's grace illustrious king of Scotland, by consent of the community of that kingdom . . .

This was perhaps even applicable shortly after the death of Andrew Moray in late November 1297. Just a few months after his emergence 'from his den', William Wallace had been elevated in social status to knight and was acknowledged as sole military and political commander in Scotland in the name of his King, John Balliol. In the hierarchical, aristocratic world of medieval state and martial affairs, this was a phenomenal achievement.

It could be argued that William Wallace's rapid rise to military and political power was made possible partly by the failures of the English in Scotland. Certainly, Scottish resistance, in general, had been aided not only by a mixture of insensitive political and economic policies imposed by the new English administration after 1296, but also a rather complacent military strategy supposedly aimed at crushing the growing opposition from May 1297. Resistance in 1297 seemed most unlikely given the apparent ease and thoroughness of the English victory and takeover in 1296. The symbolic removal of Scottish regalia, especially the Stone of Destiny, added to the actual expulsion of the Scottish King and the chief families involved in Scottish central and local government, left few rallying points for future opposition. However, Edward I's policy in 1297 of using all resources at his disposal in all lands under his direct rule – and this now included Scotland – to maintain his hold over Gascony and launch a major campaign in Flanders against the French King had unforeseen consequences in Scotland. A kingdom that had just lost its king, and independent status, suddenly felt the harsh realities of direct rule. A large sum of over £5,000 was soon raised from Scotland for use outside the country, and this was achieved through compulsory seizure of a major economic asset, wool. A rumour was reported by Scottish nobles in July 1297 that

> . . . they were told for a certainty that the king would have seized all the middle people of Scotland to send them beyond the Scottish sea in his army, to their great damage and destruction . . .

This sparked widespread unrest, as such policies affected most classes in Scottish society. When similar plans called forth political opposition to Edward I in England from both nobility and clergy in 1297, it is hardly surprising that a stronger reaction was provoked in Scotland where exactions also emphasised the impact of loss of independence.

The fact that Edward I gave full priority to warfare against the French in 1297 had repercussions for the manner in which the English governed Scotland. The English records of 1297 show how little attention (and regard) Edward I and his chief advisers gave to Scotland. In this context, the remark that Edward I is reported (by Thomas Gray in his *Scalacronica*) to have made as he gave custody of Scotland to John Warenne, Earl of Surrey, in 1296 may be accurate: 'When you get rid of a turd, you do a good job.' Lack of enthusiasm, and even contempt, for the detailed administrative consolidation that was necessary after the English victory over the Scots in 1296 was as evident in Warenne's actions as Edward's words. The *Guisborough Chronicle* provides us with some details about this:

> The earl of Warenne, to whom our king had committed the care and custody of the whole kingdom of Scotland, because of the awful weather said that he could not stay there and keep his health. He stayed in England, but in the northern part, and sluggishly pursued [the exiling of the] enemy, which was the root of our later difficulty . . .

The Guisborough chronicler also notes that Hugh Cressingham, the King's Treasurer in Scotland, had failed to construct the stone wall that the King had ordered to be built on the new rampart at Berwick, the headquarters of the English administration. The fact that many English officials did not want to be in Scotland may account for both the uncaring manner with which they implemented Edward I's policies and also their complacency towards any apparent Scottish resistance. Certainly, Hugh Cressingham soon established a reputation as a man 'who robbed too much' (*Guisborough Chronicle*). Justiciar William Ormesby was accused by the same source of strenuously persecuting those who had not sworn fealty to Edward I; while William Heselrigg, Sheriff of Lanark, was also targeted (quite literally) by William Wallace for some offence committed against the Wallace family.

Hugh Cressingham, whose frequent letters to Edward I are our main source for suggestions of the build-up of resistance in Scotland, reflects the English King's opinion that the surrender of the forces led by James Stewart, Robert Wishart, Bishop of Glasgow, and Robert Bruce would be the key to the ending of Scottish resistance:

> Sire, the letter says that if you had the earl of Carrick [Bruce], the Steward of Scotland, and his brother (who, as you understand, are the supporters of the insurrection) . . . you would think your business done.

This view seems to have been shared by Henry Percy and Robert Clifford who were in charge of the English forces to which Stewart, Wishart and Bruce capitulated at Irvine (Ayrshire) in July 1297. According to Cressingham's letter to Edward I,

> . . . we would have made an expedition on the said Thursday, had it not been for Sir Henry Percy and Sir Robert Clifford, who arrived on the Wednesday evening in that town [Roxburgh], and made known to those of your people who were there, that they had received to your peace all the enemies on this side of the Scottish sea.

Percy and Clifford ignored Cressingham's advice to attack enemies of the English north of the Forth or pursue William Wallace who had 'a large company in the forest of Selkirk'. The unsatisfactory outcome, as far as Cressingham was concerned, was that:

> . . . no expedition should be made until the earl's [Warenne's] arrival; and thus matters have gone to sleep, and each of us went away to his own residence . . .

Cressingham's increasing worries in this period of hectic letter-writing, i.e. the last week in July 1297, were further reflected in his next correspondence:

> . . . not a penny could be raised in your [realm of Scotland by any means] until my lord the earl of Warenne shall enter into your land and compel the people of the country by force and sentences of law.

His statement that Scotland was, by this time, virtually ungovernable without speedy and decisive military action is forthright:

> But, sire, let it not displease you, by far the greater part of your counties of the realm of Scotland are still unprovided with keepers; and some have given up their bailiwicks, and others neither will nor dare return; and in some counties the Scots have appointed and established bailiffs and ministers, so that no county is in proper order, excepting Berwick and Roxburgh, and this only recently. But, sire, all this shall be speedily amended, by the grace of God, and the arrival of the lord earl, Sir Henry Percy, and Sir Robert Clifford, and the others of your council.

Further delay in English military action occurred, no doubt, in early August as a result of Edward I's proposal for Earl Warenne to join him on the continent (clearly still the King's priority) and be replaced in Scotland

This view shows an area that was once Rothbury Forest. This area together with Selkirk Forest (the ancient Ettrick Forest) in southern Scotland were of strategic importance to William Wallace as he prepared his army for the fight against the English.

Overleaf, background image: Castle Urquhart, situated on Strone Point on the western shore of Loch Ness.

THE MORAYS

The family of Moray (later Murray) was descended from a Fleming called Freskin, who was given Duffus near Elgin by David I (1124–53) as part of a planned crown settlement in this important region of Scotland. In the early thirteenth century, the family took the surname 'Moray' or 'de Moravia' as a result of their growing importance in the area. They were promoted into territorial, administrative and ecclesiastical offices to further royal interests and loosen the grip of the earls of Caithness. By the mid-thirteenth century the Morays held the earldom of Sutherland, the lordships of Duffus (near Elgin)

Duffus Castle. Freskin, the founder of the family 'Moray', 'de Moravia' (a name adopted as a surname in the early thirteenth century), received Duffus near Elgin as part of his grant from David I in the twelfth century. His family was responsible for the initial 'motte' (mound) at Duffus.

Fortrose Cathedral. Andrew Moray, joint leader of Scottish resistance in northern Scotland during 1297, was gravely injured in the Battle of Stirling Bridge (22 September 1297) and only survived for a few months. He was buried at Fortrose Cathedral.

Loch Ness. Andrew Moray captured Urquhart Castle, on the western shore of Loch Ness, during his campaign of resistance in northern Scotland. Urquhart presided over the strategic route along the Great Glen to Inverness. Control over Loch Ness was important for authority over northern Scotland.

Bothwell Castle, one of the most impressive fortifications of thirteenth-century Scotland. It was planned by Walter Moray after 1242 but was not completed before the start of the Scottish wars.

and Petty (near Inverness) as well as lands in Strathspey. Given Alexander III's anxiety to increase royal authority in the north in the second half of the thirteenth century, the Morays were more involved in royal service in this reign. Alexander Moray became Sheriff of Inverness, 1264–6 and Malcolm Moray was appointed Sheriff of Perth, 1257–89. Later, Andrew Moray was Sheriff of Ayr, and some time between 1289 and 1296 gained the office of Justiciar of Scotia, the most important political and administrative position in Scotland. The family were further empowered by marriage links with the Comyns, the most dominant political group in thirteenth-century Scotland. The Morays were powerful representatives of Scottish government and the Scottish kingship of John Balliol. It is intriguing to speculate what leadership role Andrew Moray, son of the Justiciar, would have played in the Scottish patriot movement if he had not been fatally wounded at the Battle of Stirling Bridge in 1297.

by Brian Fitz Alan at less cost. Edward I planned to move more senior figures and additional resources to his continental campaign. He clearly thought that Scottish opposition would scatter with a show of English force (however late), as it had done in 1296 at Dunbar and in 1297 at Irvine. Brian Fitz Alan, however, was as reluctant as Warenne to take on responsibility for Scotland, as detailed by him in a letter to Edward I, 5 August 1297:

> I do not think that I in my poverty can be able either well or honourably to keep the land in peace to your profit and honour, when such a nobleman as the earl cannot well keep it in peace for what he receives from you.

When Fitz Alan tried to bargain for a better financial deal – that he would take custody upon the same terms as Warenne had – Edward refused and Warenne eventually continued as Keeper of Scotland. Cressingham gave another warning early in August that

> . . . peace on the other side of the Scottish sea is still in obscurity, as it is said, as to the doings of the earls who are there [the Comyns, one Earl of Buchan and the other Lord of Badenoch, released from an English prison to pacify the north] . . .

The fact, also, that Wallace was strong enough to lay siege to Dundee Castle and that he and Moray were able to move around large areas of the country that were not under firm English administrative control, still had little impact on the official English conduct of their campaign against Scottish resistance.

By late August 1297, Warenne had at last reached Berwick and the forces of Cressingham and Warenne advanced from Berwick to Stirling, which was reached in the first week of September. It was important to consolidate control over Stirling, the most strategic crossing point of the Forth and to confront the forces of Andrew Moray and William Wallace, which were moving without restriction north of the Forth. According to the *Lanercost Chronicle*, the Scots 'began to show themselves in rebellion' by about 8 September and this may indicate that the forces of Moray and Wallace, hitherto engaged in individual action, had combined to form a large army of resistance. The joint strength of their two groups, as well as the success that they had enjoyed up to this point, seems to have persuaded Wallace and Moray to face the English army in pitched battle rather than employ the 'hit and run' tactics of the ambush. John of Fordun confirms the fact that Wallace led by fear as much as popular support. This is particularly reflected in his threat to the burgesses of Dundee who were left to continue to besiege the English in Dundee Castle:

Stirling Castle, the key stronghold that linked northern and southern Scotland. Control over this castle was important for asserting authority over the whole of Scotland. This is reflected by the Battle of Stirling Bridge (1297), the three-month siege of 1304 and the Battle of Bannockburn (1314)

William . . . straightway intrusted the care and charge of the siege of the castle to the burgesses of that town on pain of life and limb . . .

Fordun also indicates that Wallace's control had a much wider base:

> . . . in a short time, by force, and by dint of his prowess, [he] brought all the magnates of Scotland under his sway, whether they would or not. Such of the magnates, moreover, as did not thankfully obey his commands he took and browbeat . . .

These sentiments seem to run counter to the notion that Wallace was, at this stage, a frontman acting on behalf of James Stewart and Bishop Robert Wishart. Who then was leader of Scottish resistance to the English in early September 1297?

It has been seen that opposition to the English administration in Scotland was widespread in the north as well as the south. Individuals named in the sources as being actively involved in the revolt during 1297 were, apart from William Wallace, Andrew Moray, William Douglas, James Stewart, Robert Wishart, Bishop of Glasgow, Robert Bruce, Earl of Carrick, Duncan Macdougall, Macduff of Fife and his two sons, John Stewart and Alexander Lindsay. In addition, Hugh Cressingham and English chroniclers suspected that the leading members of the Comyns were not acting in Edward's interests in helping to put down (as they had promised) the rebellions in Scotland following their release from English prisons. The English officials had no proof that the Comyns were siding openly with the Scots before Stirling Bridge, though Moray, a kinsman of the Comyns, would not have been able to gather as many supporters without, at least, the clandestine backing of the Comyn-dominated local administration of the north.

It could also be said to be true that without at least the tacit approval of the Stewarts and Bishop Wishart Wallace too would have struggled to gain local recruits in central and south-western Scotland. The Lanercost and Guisborough chroniclers assert throughout their narratives of the 1297 revolt that Wishart and Stewart masterminded the revolt and Wallace's actions. In early July 1297, Robert Wishart, James Stewart and Robert Bruce, Earl of Carrick, came out in open opposition to Edward I. In their company were

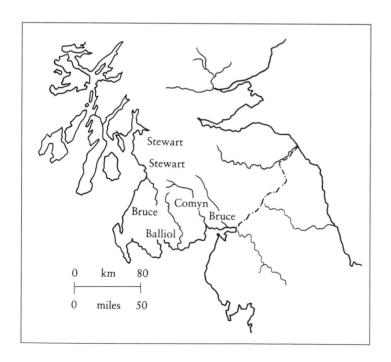

Noble power bases in south-west Scotland.

James Stewart's brother, John, Alexander Lindsay and William Douglas (who had participated with William Wallace in the attack on Justiciar William Ormesby at Scone). They were defeated – or more accurately, they capitulated to the English forces of Henry Percy and Robert Clifford at Irvine on 7 July.

The fact that Wishart, Stewart and Bruce had not completed the terms of the surrender a month afterwards has suggested to historians that they were engaged in an exercise of deliberate procrastination in order to assist the other revolts in Scotland. It was clear from the negotiations that Wishart, Stewart and Bruce saw themselves as leaders of the Scottish political community and that Edward I and his officials also considered them to be the leaders of Scottish resistance. Perhaps this official view is reflected in the unambiguous verdict given by the English chroniclers. However, the accepted theory of political rule in Scotland was being tested by the reality of military leadership of a nationwide anti-English resistance movement. Traditional political leaders such as the Comyns and their allies in 1296 and Wishart, Stewart and Bruce in 1297 did not feel that they could match a large English army and, therefore, at Dunbar (1296) and Irvine (1297) surrender terms were soon sought. They had made a political point and were seeking a political solution. Andrew Moray, William Douglas and William Wallace had less to lose than Stewarts, Comyns and Bruces by taking a purely military, and certainly less vacillating, approach. Their aim was simply to remove the English from the country.

The three most successful resistance leaders – Moray, Douglas and Wallace – had different backgrounds. Moray and Douglas were sons of noblemen from families linked by a relationship since the late twelfth century. Wallace, on the other hand, was the son of a knight. Moray had perhaps better credentials for leadership being from a family strongly associated with Scottish government and related by marriage to the Comyns who dominated that government. Wallace and Douglas had reputations as troublemakers. Wallace, though in the following of the Stewarts, had probably been an outlaw since 1296 and, unlike most of the Stewart retinue, had not sworn fealty to Edward I. William Douglas, though from an aristocratic family, had a reputation for rash actions and, despite having his goods restored to him after his surrender of Berwick Castle to Edward I, according to the *Guisborough Chronicle* he 'turned robber working with a robber'. Douglas was present with Wallace during the attack on the Justiciar William Ormesby at Scone and was also with Stewart, Wishart and Bruce at Irvine. He was with Moray and Wallace at Stirling Bridge on 11 September 1297. Unlike Stewart, Wishart and Bruce after ceding at Irvine, Douglas remained uncooperative, as a letter to Edward I from Hugh Cressingham, 24 July 1297, reveals:

Dear sire, because sir William Douglas has not kept the covenants which he made with sir Henry de Percy, he is in your castle of Berwick, in my keeping, and he is still very savage and abusive . . .

After Irvine, only Moray and Wallace remained to lead Scottish resistance. The Guisborough chronicler's description of William Wallace's support probably applies equally to that of Moray:

The common folk of the land followed him as their leader and ruler; the retainers of the great lords adhered to him; and even though the lords themselves were present with the English king in body, at heart they were on the opposite side.

In late July, Moray was described as having a 'large body of rogues' (letter of the Bishop of Aberdeen and others to Edward I, 25 July 1297) in Speyside, while at the same time, Wallace 'lay there with a large company (and does so still) in the forest of Selkirk' (letter from Hugh Cressingham to Edward I, 23 July 1297). The successes of Moray and Wallace, in northern and southern Scotland respectively, had separated the traditional

Rothbury Forest, Eddingham. This forest was used as a base by William Wallace as he organised the invasion of northern England in October 1297.

Cambuskenneth Abbey, Stirling. The ruins of the abbey, founded in about 1147 by David I of Scotland, are overlooked by Stirling Castle and the town. Edward I visited the abbey in 1303/4.

political leaders from their retainers and followers. Could the Comyns, Stewarts and Bruce be anything more than supportive bystanders in early September as the English forces approached Stirling? How significant was the fact that Robert Wishart's considerable influence had been removed by his imprisonment in Roxburgh Castle (he was released on parole only in spring 1298)? Indeed, the *Lanercost Chronicle* suggests that Wishart had primary responsibility for the rebellion of 1297, ahead of James Stewart, referring to the Bishop as 'ever foremost in treason'. As Bishop of Glasgow, he had the most effective means, through the parish priests of his diocese, of disseminating the message of revolt. Certainly, Edward I's subsequent complaint to the Pope that 'it was by abetment and counsel of the prelates and clerks of their land that the Scots rose with William Wallace' (cited in C. Kightly, *Folk Heroes of Britain* [London, Thames & Hudson, 1982]) and his later treatment of Wishart indicates that the Bishop bore a heavy responsibility for the inception of Scottish resistance.

The Battle of Stirling Bridge was fought on 11 September 1297. The English forces of Cressingham and Warenne had reached the English-held Stirling Castle during the first week of September. The Scottish force, led by Moray and Wallace, was at Dundee on about 8 September and had to march 50 miles to reach Stirling. On 9 September, before the Scots reached Stirling, James Stewart, Malcolm, Earl of Lennox, and other Scottish nobles approached the English army. According to the *Guisborough Chronicle*, the Scottish lords:

> . . . came in to ask us [the English] whether we would delay a little while, to see if they could pacify their retainers and the other Scots folk in any way. So we gave them until 10th September when they returned saying that they could not do as they had hoped, but that they would nevertheless come to join us the next day with 40 knights.

The *Lanercost Chronicle*, rather more explicitly, accuses James Stewart of treachery:

> . . . the Steward treacherously said to them [the English] – 'It is not expedient to set in motion so great a multitude on account of a single rascal; send with me a few picked men, and I will bring him to you dead or alive.'

Both English chroniclers continue to write as if, at this stage, as at the beginning of the 1297 revolt, Stewart was masterminding the military activities of Wallace. The English writers also focus on Wallace rather than Andrew Moray. The reality was probably different, especially after the abject surrender, without a fight, of Stewart, Wishart and Bruce, self-styled

The Seal of John Moray, c. 1250. It depicts, in a flowery meadow, a bull passant to sinister (left) with a star of six points over its back. (By permission of the Court of the Lord Lyon.)

leaders of the community of the realm, at Irvine in early July. With some of his associates at Irvine, namely William Douglas and Robert Wishart, in prison, Stewart must, at best, have been 'on probation', i.e. needing to be on his best behaviour, as far as the English commanders were concerned. It is probable that he was making a token gesture of arbitration in keeping with his political status; it is possible that he wished to persuade Moray and Wallace that a pitched battle with an English army superior in cavalry and larger in number was foolish – that had been his own policy in 1296, following Dunbar, and in 1297 at Irvine. It is unlikely that he had, at this time, sufficient military credibility to offer advice to Moray and Wallace – and have such counsel accepted. It is most improbable, therefore, that he had the military boldness to lure the English over the bridge at Stirling to allow the army of Moray and Wallace to ambush them, as suggested by the Lanercost chronicler. Delaying tactics, as after Irvine, was the most that Stewart could offer Wallace and Moray.

Details of the Battle of Stirling Bridge are chiefly drawn from the Guisborough chronicler who may have been party to an eyewitness account of the Yorkshire nobleman, Marmaduke Thweng. This did not, however, stop Walter of Guisborough from greatly exaggerating the figures for those involved in the battle. He gave the English numbers as 1,000 horsemen (cavalry) and 50,000 footmen (many were Welsh), with the Scottish army comprising 180 horsemen (cavalry) and 40,000 footmen. Hugh Cressingham wrote to Edward I on 23 July that he had mustered from Northumberland 300 horsemen and 10,000 footmen, so this is a minimum figure. What is clear is that the English army had greater numbers in total and a striking superiority in cavalry – and it was unheard of, at this time, that such a large mounted force could be defeated. Stewart was a cautious pragmatist rather than a coward.

The Scottish force had gathered on the slopes of the Abbey Craig, the site of the Wallace Monument today. Their position was a mile north of the original bridge over the Forth. North of the bridge was a causeway with fairly soft ground on either side of it. On the south side of the Forth, half a mile from the bridge, lay Stirling Castle. In the days before the battle, it seems that the English were anticipating a Scottish surrender, as at Irvine and Dunbar, and were prepared to wait for it. Even when Lennox wounded an English foot soldier as he left the English camp with Stewart, on 9 September, to negotiate with Moray and Wallace, Warenne ignored the call for instant vengeance, as reported in the *Guisborough Chronicle*:

> Let us wait tonight, and see whether they keep their promise in the morning; then we shall better be able to demand satisfaction for this insult . . .

The events of the morning of 10 September reveal, yet again, the lackadaisical, disorganised approach of the English commanders, as well as their belief that the Scottish would capitulate eventually. The *Guisborough Chronicle* continues:

> Thus it was ordered that everyone should be ready to pass over the bridge of Stirling the next morning, and more than 5,000 of our infantry, with many Welshmen, did in fact then cross it; but they were called back again, because the earl had not yet woken from his sleep . . .

When he did awake, Warenne still showed a complete lack of urgency. As the Guisborough chronicler reveals, he put chivalry before practicality and 'made several new knights':

> Meanwhile our infantry was crossing the bridge a second time, but they were ordered back yet again, for the Stewart and Lennox were seen riding in with only a small retinue, and not with the 40 knights they had promised. We thought, therefore, that they must be the bearers of good tidings . . . but they only made excuses saying they could neither persuade their followers to submit nor even obtain horses or weapons from them . . .

Stirling Old Bridge. The bridge that gave its name to the Battle of Stirling Bridge was a wooden one close to (a little upstream of) the present 'old bridge', which was built in the sixteenth century. According to the Seal of the Burgh of Stirling, the original wooden bridge had eight spans.

The impression given by the English chroniclers and the Scottish chronicler John of Fordun was that the Scottish lords had lost control over their retinues to Moray and Wallace. It is interesting that, even at this stage, Warenne sought a Scottish surrender and so, according to the Guisborough chronicler, he sent across two Dominican friars to 'that robber Wallace' to 'see if by any chance he wished to put forward any peace terms'. Wallace's unequivocal reply, no doubt voiced previously to Stewart and Lennox, was as follows (*Guisborough Chronicle*):

'Go back and tell your people that we have not come here for peace; we are ready, rather, to fight to avenge ourselves and free our country. Let them come up to us as soon as they like, and we shall prove this in their very beards.'

When this reply was heard, the reaction of the rasher men on the English side once more showed a complacent disregard for the smaller Scottish force: 'Let us go up to them at once; their numbers are but small.' (*Guisborough Chronicle*). This complacency with regard to the Scottish strength of numbers came, of course, from the top of the English command. Cressingham was keenly aware of Edward I's shortage of money and had already ordered home the troops that Henry Percy had brought to Stirling from Cumbria and Lancashire, as recorded by the Guisborough chronicler:

> . . . saying that our army was already quite large enough, and that there was no point either in putting themselves to needless trouble or in spending more of the king's treasure than they could help . . .

There then followed debate in the army about how the English attack on the Scottish forces would be conducted. According to the Guisborough chronicler again, Richard Lundie, a Scottish knight who had come over to the English side at Irvine, gave good advice:

> 'My lords, if we cross that bridge now, we are all dead men. For we can only go over two abreast, and the enemy are already formed up: they can charge down on us together whenever they wish. There is, however, a ford not far from here, where 60 men can cross at a time. Give me 500 cavalrymen, then, and a small body of infantry, and we will outflank the enemy and attack them from behind: while we are doing that, the earl and the rest of the army will be able to cross the bridge in perfect safety.' But our leaders refused to accept this sound advice, declaring that it would be unsafe to divide our army.

It is probable that, at the outset, Moray and Wallace did not have a strategy to ambush the English at the bridge. After their march from Dundee, it is unlikely that they were in a position to strike against the English when they twice crossed the bridge on the morning of 10 September. However, the rather confused manoeuvrings of the English army during this morning must have given them the idea (and the confidence) to launch an attack on the English when they eventually made their way across the bridge on 11 September.

It is in keeping with the conduct of the English campaign against Scottish resistance in 1297 that the eventual decision to cross the narrow bridge at Stirling was taken by the militarily inexperienced Hugh Cressingham, and for financial rather than military reasons. Even worse, Earl Warenne allowed himself to accept the Treasurer's dubious judgement (*Guisborough Chronicle*):

> 'It will do us no good, my lord earl, either to go on bickering like this or to waste the king's money by vain manoeuvres. So let us cross over right away, and do our duty as we are bound to do.'

The worst fears of Richard Lundie were realised (*Guisborough Chronicle*):

The Battle of Stirling Bridge – William Hole's nineteenth-century mural of the battle. (Reproduced by permission of the Scottish National Portrait Gallery.)

Thus (amazing though it is to relate, and terrible as was to be its outcome) all these experienced men, though they knew the enemy was ready at hand, began to pass over a bridge so narrow that even two horsemen could scarcely and with much difficulty ride side by side . . . and so they did all the morning, without let or hindrance, until the vanguard was on one side of the river and the remainder of the army on the other. There was, indeed, no better place in all the land to deliver the English into the hands of the Scots, and so many into the power of so few.

According to the *Guisborough Chronicle*, which is supported by the *Lanercost Chronicle*, the Scots waited until as many English had crossed the bridge as they thought they could successfully attack. Moray and Wallace and their forces then moved down from the hill:

. . . sending meanwhile a large body of spearmen to block the [northern] end of the bridge so that no English could either come across or retire over it.

Later writers elaborated on the ambush, with Thomas Gray reporting in *Scalacronica* that Wallace 'caused the bridge to be broken'. Even more elaborately, Blind Harry's *The Wallace* tells how Wallace employed a 'cunning carpenter, by name John Wright' to sabotage the bridge by cutting through the main beam and supporting it with a wooden pin. Wright, hiding under the bridge 'in a close cradle' knocked out the pin on hearing a blast from Wallace's horn, which signalled that sufficient English troops were on the bridge. Such a detailed plan was probably not feasible and the more contemporary and very full account of the Guisborough chronicler states that the bridge remained intact, and this is a more preferable version.

In the *Guisborough Chronicle* it is reported that 100 English knights and 5,000 infantry were killed either by Scottish spearmen or by drowning in the Forth. The vanguard of the English army was almost completely destroyed, while the cavalry were unable to be deployed because of the boggy turf on the north side of the bridge, the confines of the river, which surrounded them on three sides, and the pressure of the Scottish infantry. A few lightly clad infantry escaped by swimming but Sir Marmaduke Thweng, the knight who probably related his account to the Guisborough chronicler, decided to face the Scottish troops:

'My dear fellow, do not tell me to drown myself on purpose. Forget all that nonsense and follow me, and we will hack a path through the midst of them.'

Thweng succeeded but Cressingham, fatally impatient to defeat the Scots at the earliest opportunity, and the standard-bearers of both the King and Warenne were slain. The Scots made an example of the hated Treasurer, and according to the Lanercost chronicler, Wallace '. . . caused a broad strip [of skin] to be taken from the head to the heel, to make thereof a baldrick for his sword'. The Guisborough chronicler reports an equally grisly end for Cressingham: '. . . the Scots afterwards flayed his fat body, and divided strips of skin amongst them, not as holy relics, but as mockery of him . . .'. In *Scalacronica* Thomas Gray states that the Scots '. . . in token of hatred made girths of his skin.'

The English forces under Earl Warenne on the south side of the bridge saw the devastation and confusion. Warenne was unable to come to Cressingham's aid because of the narrowness of the bridge and decided to flee with a small following to Berwick. The Lanercost chronicler records that he escaped 'with difficulty', leaving Marmaduke Thweng at Stirling Castle while the rest of his army followed him to Berwick. At this late stage, with Warenne and the English army in retreat, Stewart and Lennox emerged to harry the English baggage train and all English fugitives from the battle.

The Scots suffered few casualties at Stirling Bridge but Andrew Moray, joint leader of the Scottish army, was seriously injured, and he died from his wounds in November 1297. This meant that William Wallace took an even more prominent role in the continuing Scottish campaign against the English presence. According to the *Scalacronica*, William Wallace:

> . . . followed the said Earl of Warenne in great force and skirting Berwick, arrived on Hutton Moor in order of battle; but perceiving the English arrayed to oppose him, he came no nearer to Berwick, but retired and bivouacked in Duns Park [north of Berwick].

Warenne left Berwick with Wallace's approach, leaving the town wasted before his departure. The *Scalacronica* gives a strong impression of Wallace now being in clear command of military operations:

> . . . perceiving the departure of the Earl of Warenne, sent the chevalier Henry de Haliburton to seize Berwick, and appointed others to besiege Robert de Hastings in Roxburgh Castle with a great force.

The Scots entered Berwick, the town that still lacked protective walls owing to the failure of Cressingham – perhaps for financial reasons again – to provide them. The few remaining English in the town were killed, though the castle was not surrendered and, therefore, gave refuge to some. Wallace did not advance into Northumberland but the inhabitants of the county, fearing the worst, fled in terror to Newcastle with their families, belongings and animals.

Bamburgh Castle, an important refuge for the people of northern Northumberland. The parishes of Norhamshire recorded sharp declines in tax revenues probably as a result of the damage inflicted on this area by Wallace and his army.

An invasion of northern England was not immediately forthcoming but the Northumbrians were right to fear that an offensive was imminent – the first recorded activity was on 13 October. In the weeks before this date, Wallace continued with his principal task of driving out the English from their few remaining enclaves in Scotland. Yet he had no siege weapons and though Stirling Castle, with Marmaduke Thweng as commander, soon surrendered owing to lack of provisions, Wallace was unable to take the castles at Berwick or Roxburgh.

The victory by Moray and Wallace at Stirling Bridge was, however, a huge psychological blow to the English and strengthened the position in Scotland of the only two successful leaders of Scottish resistance. The fact that the commanders of the army of the Scottish realm were already seen as the effective rulers of Scotland is indicated in a formal document dated 11 October 1297. Andrew Moray and William Wallace wrote to the mayors and people of the towns of Lübeck and Hamburg that Scottish ports were now open and safe for access for their merchants:

> Andrew de Moray and William Wallace, leaders of the army, and the community of the realm, to their wise and discreet beloved friends the mayors and common people of Lübeck and of Hamburg . . . we willingly enter into an undertaking with you asking you to have it announced to your merchants that they can have safe access to all

ports of the Scottish kingdom with their merchants because the kingdom of Scotland, thanks be to God, has been recovered by battle from the power of the English. Farewell. Given at Haddington 11th October 1297 . . .

This reveals that if the army commanded by Moray and Wallace at Stirling Bridge was the 'army of the kingdom of Scotland' its leaders now had control over clerks knowledgeable of the workings of the Scottish royal chancery. This document, one of only four surviving that emanated from Wallace himself, reveals that Scotland was, in practice, being run by its military leaders. They, however, had a clear grasp of economic necessities – their regime needed money, through trade, to be able to maintain its independence and the letter to Lübeck and Hamburg was probably one of many sent to Scotland's trading partners to encourage a resumption of trade. A postscript to the letter contains a further request to the mayors of Lübeck and Hamburg:

> . . . to agree to promote the business of John Burnet and John Frere, our merchants, just as you may wish us to promote the business of your merchants . . .

This definitely shows Wallace in a rather different light to 'outlaw', 'robber' or 'guerrilla leader'. Instead, he is portrayed as a man capable of grasping the economic detail necessary for political leadership.

Another letter of 7 November, this time a letter of protection issued by Andrew Moray and William Wallace, sheds further light on Wallace's political position. Here Moray and Wallace describe themselves as

> . . . commanders of the army of the kingdom of Scotland, in the name of the famous prince the lord John, by God's grace illustrious king of Scotland, by consent of the community of that realm.

It is clear what Wallace stood for and it is also evident from the order of their names in the letter that Andrew Moray was still regarded at the time, though gravely wounded, as the senior of the two. At some stage in the period between 7 November 1297 and 29 March 1298, William Wallace was knighted to give him, in theory, the same noble status as Moray, Stewart, Comyn and Bruce. It is stated in the Charter of William Wallace to Alexander Scrymgeour, 29 March 1298, that he acquired the title of

> . . . knight, Guardian of the kingdom of Scotland and commander of its army, in the name of the famous prince the lord John, by God's grace illustrious king of Scotland, by consent of the community of that kingdom.

By this time, if not earlier – Moray died in November 1297 – Wallace had become sole military and political commander of Scotland. He invested Alexander Scrymgeour with the Constabulary of Dundee as a reward for carrying the royal standard in battle. In practice, Moray and Wallace formally resurrected the principle of Guardianship soon after their victory at Stirling Bridge. The Guardians had held the nation in trust for its rightful monarch between 1286 and 1291 and, as has been seen, upheld the tenet of an independent Scotland through the Treaty of Birgham (1290). Moray and Wallace still regarded John Balliol, forcibly deposed by Edward I and still in captivity in England, as the lawful King of Scotland. They acted in his name and used his seal in government.

It is important to be aware that through their military successes before Stirling Bridge, but principally in the battle there, Moray and Wallace had eclipsed the traditional ruling families of Scotland. The events after Stirling Bridge cause us to question the strongly held view that is expressed through the *Guisborough Chronicle* and the *Lanercost Chronicle*: that Wallace was merely the military arm of the political resistance masterminded by Bishop Robert Wishart and Wallace's feudal lord, James Stewart.

If this had been the case, why did Wallace after Stirling Bridge not hand over the reigns of political power to James Stewart and Robert Wishart, who had clearly seen themselves, with Robert Bruce, as the leaders of the Scottish political community in early July 1297? Why did Andrew Moray not defer to his kinsmen, the Comyns, who had returned to Scotland by this time, although they were still not openly backing Scottish resistance? Of the traditional aristocratic ruling elite in Scotland, the Comyns appear to have been the least involved in the Battle of Stirling Bridge and its aftermath. They had pledged to put down the rebellion in the north of Scotland and, despite the doubts of Hugh Cressingham, were still believed to be loyal to Edward I as late as 26 September 1297. The presence of John Comyn, the younger, heir of the main Badenoch branch of the family, in Edward I's army in Flanders may have dissuaded the Comyns from an open position. Their attitude may have changed by March 1298 when John Comyn, the younger, was among the Scots who deserted Edward's army and sought help at the French court. Robert Wishart, imprisoned in Roxburgh Castle, which was still in English hands, was unable to assume political control, even if asked. Yet James Stewart had, after the Battle of Stirling Bridge had been won, joined in with the attack on the English army's baggage train. He would have been the natural, experienced political leader, a former Guardian. However, it is clear that before Stirling Bridge, the traditional Scottish political leaders, such as Stewart, had lost the support of their retainers because of their cautious political (and military) stance. Moray and Wallace had the backing of the retainers and chief military adherents of the major Scottish nobles.

The Seal of William Lamberton, Bishop of St Andrews (1297–1328). An immensely significant personality in the Scottish patriot cause, Lamberton was elected to the premier bishopric in Scotland when William Wallace was in political control of Scotland after the Battle of Stirling Bridge. The seal (dated 1309–10) shows the bishop in a canopied niche, front face with mitre, his right hand raised in benediction, his left holding a crozier. (By permission of the Court of the Lord Lyon.)

Moray and Wallace were certainly competent enough to assume the political mantle that Stirling Bridge brought them. However, their judgements have tended to be overshadowed, especially in English eyes, by Wallace's invasion of northern England between mid-October and 22 November 1297. Some of their early decisions included negotiations with foreign ports, the replacement of a key figure in the political as well as ecclesiastical life of Scotland following the death (in France) of the Bishop of St Andrews, William Fraser, in 1297 – William Lamberton was elected at Wallace's behest on 3 November – and the holding of parliaments.

The Scottish invasion of northern England is perhaps the best-documented episode of William Wallace's career and is discussed in depth in C.J. McNamee, 'William Wallace's Invasion of Northern England in 1297', *Northern History* XXXVI (1990), 40–58, to which the following section is greatly indebted. The earliest reference to Scottish

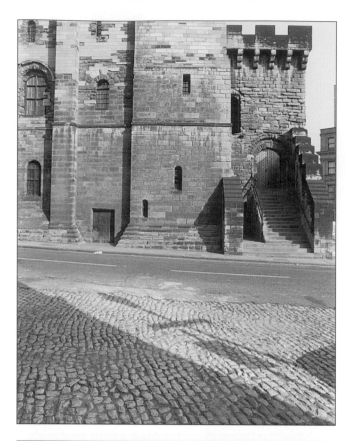

Newcastle, the castle. Newcastle prepared to be attacked on several occasions in 1297 but it was too strong for Wallace's forces. The castle site was considerably affected by the arrival of the railway in 1849. The main medieval remains comprise the keep (late twelfth century) and the gatehouse, Black Gate (mid-thirteenth century).

Newcastle walls. Little remains of the 2-mile circuit (started in 1265) that was praised for its strength and magnificence in the sixteenth century. Newcastle was not fully enclosed by walls in 1297 and no doubt this fact caused panic at the time and ensured that the work was speedily completed.

Alnwick Castle. The garrison here seemed to offer William Wallace's invasion force at least some opposition in 1297. Perhaps, as a result, the Scots devastated the town. Alnwick's defensive fortifications were considerably developed under the Percy family in the fourteenth century but were still strong enough in 1297 to resist Wallace. The castle was not taken by Wallace's forces

Carlisle Castle, which defied William Wallace in 1297 and Robert Bruce in 1315. Given Wallace's army's lack of experience in siege warfare, castles could only be taken through either surprise or subterfuge. Usually, Wallace avoided well-defended strongholds such as Newcastle or Carlisle.

activity in northern England concerns the burning of Felton Mill (about 7 miles from Rothbury) on about 13 October. The Guisborough chronicler refers to Scottish raids in Northumberland on 18 October but the major incursion did not take place until 11 November. This date probably marks the involvement of William Wallace and a more organised invading force after scattered raids by Scots caught up in the euphoria of the victory at Stirling Bridge. Another possible motive for the random assaults and the more regulated invasion was the lack of provisions in Scotland. The fifteenth-century Scottish chronicler, Walter Bower, refers to the shortage of corn in Scotland as a result of poor weather. Perhaps, too, the harvesting season in Scotland had been badly disrupted by the fighting as Moray and Wallace had gathered large numbers of men willing to fight for their cause. Wallace and Moray would have known that Edward I was out of the country and not able, for a while, to mount a counter-offensive to avenge Stirling Bridge. Warenne had, in fact, retreated from Berwick to York. There could not be a better opportunity for plunder and to consolidate assets for the battles ahead. An outline of the invasion route is given in the *Lanercost Chronicle*:

After these events the Scots entered Northumberland in strength, wasting all the land, committing arson, pillage, and murder, and advancing as far as the town of Newcastle; from which, however, they turned aside and entered the county of Carlisle. They there did as they had done in Northumberland, destroying everything, then returned into

Cockermouth. Scottish raids reached almost to Cockermouth Castle in the west during 1297. Again Wallace tended to avoid besieging strongholds.

Northumberland to lay waste more completely what they had left at first; and re-entered Scotland on the feast of St Cecilia, Virgin and Martyr, without, however, having been able to capture any castle either in England or Scotland

Once again rather more detail about the Scottish invasion is to be obtained from the *Guisborough Chronicle*. The Scots are described as:

. . . splitting up into separate troops, and sending out scouts before them, came suddenly and secretly into Northumberland . . . whose inhabitants, thinking that the enemy would not now come, had foolishly returned to their homes. Quickly spreading all over the county, they slew many and carried off much spoil: they set up a camp in Rothbury Forest (near the border) and came and went just as they liked, for there was no one to scare them off. At that time the service of God totally ceased in all the monasteries and churches between Newcastle and Carlisle, for all the monks, canons and priests fled before the face of the Scots as did nearly all the people. And thus the enemy went on plundering and burning . . . with no opposition save from our men in Alnwick castle and a few other strong places . . . until about 11 November, when they gathered themselves together and moved off, harrying as they went.

Brough Castle. It is probable that William Wallace bypassed this castle and reached as far as Bowes before abandoning his march into the bishopric of Durham.

Overleaf: Derwentwater. Wallace's army did cause some damage in the area of Bassenthwaite Lake and may have passed by Keswick and Derwentwater on the way to Stainmore and the bishopric of Durham before this expedition was abandoned.

The ancient stone circle at Castlerigg, Keswick, would have overlooked the probable route taken by William Wallace as he passed through this area.

The Scots progressed into northern Cumbria and approached Carlisle, recently repaired and too strong for an army lacking in siege weaponry. According to the Guisborough chronicler, Wallace sent in:

> . . . some shameless priest who said, 'William the Conqueror, whom I serve, commands you to give up this town and castle without bloodshed: then you may leave unharmed with all your goods. But if you do not instantly obey him, he will attack and kill you all.'

In this case, Wallace was not a 'conqueror' at Carlisle and instead moved through Inglewood Forest almost as far as Cockermouth. The Scots did not reach Westmorland but did contemplate advancing into the bishopric of Durham. This suggests that they reached a point near Bowes on Stainmoor where they were stopped (as many travellers have been) by snow storms, but also the rumour (probably false) that 'an immense number of Durham folk were ready to meet them in arms' (*Guisborough Chronicle*). The Scots then, perhaps on about 18 November, decided to march back to Scotland via Tynedale. Now joined by the notoriously independent and undisciplined men of Galloway, Wallace used Hexham Priory as his base for two days while his men ravaged the lower Tyne valley almost to the gates of Newcastle itself. Just as Berwick's town walls had not been completed by Hugh Cressingham, so the town walls around Newcastle were unfinished. Its castle, rather than the walls, remained its greatest strength and a garrison was maintained at the castle from 6 November until February – it consisted of 6 men at arms, 60 crossbowmen and 40 archers. The Scots did not attack, Wallace's forces returning north to Scotland while the men from

The South Tyne valley was ravaged by William Wallace's army in 1297 from their base in Hexham. Bywell and Corbridge were particularly affected.

Galloway, having received their share of the plunder, probably returned home through Tynedale.

The degree of estimated devastation in northern England has tended to depend on the location of the English chronicle source – the further south the chronicler, the more extreme the horrors of the Scottish invasion of 1297. William Rishanger reports that:

> Driving together English men and women, the vile Scots tied them with whips and scorpions until they dropped. They even snatched up babes from the cradle or their mothers' breasts and cut them open, and they burned alive many children in schools and churches.

The author of *Song on the Scottish Wars* wrote, in similar tone, of Scottish atrocities:

> . . . the troops of the Scots reduce the estates of many to cinders, William Wallace is the leader of these savages; the rejoicings of fools breed increase of griefs. – To increase the wickedness which they had hitherto perpetrated, these wicked men deliver Alnwick to the flames, they run about on every side like madmen . . . Many ask each other how it happened, that Newminster was not touched by the fire. The monks promise gifts, but they do not fulfil their promise; as

The site of Newminster Abbey. In the absence of English military assistance, Newminster Abbey, a Cistercian daughter-house of Fountains Abbey (Yorkshire), tried to bargain with the Scottish forces under Wallace but the abbey was looted after their promise of gifts was not fulfilled.

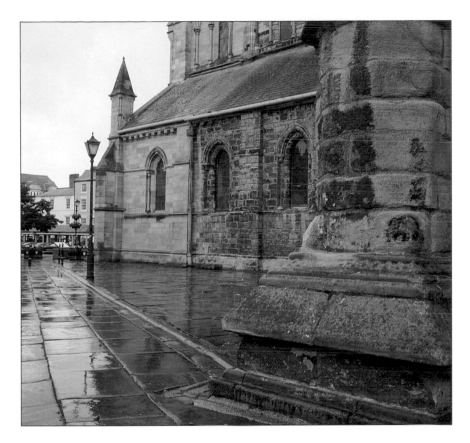

Hexham Priory. Wallace used the priory as a base for two days and it proved difficult to control the notoriously wild men of Galloway. There was some looting at the priory.

there was need, so was the thing carried into effect. – On this account they led away captive the prior of the monastery, whom they then found; having carried away the goods, they left the houses empty.

Songs recorded in the *Lanercost Chronicle* reflect contemporary opinion on raids on Lanercost Priory and also Hexham Priory:

Of the Impiety of the Scots
O Scottish race! God's holy shrines have been defiled by thee,
His sacred temples thou hast burnt, O crying shame to see!
Think not that thou for these misdeeds shalt punishment avoid,
For Hexham's famous sanctuary polluted and destroyed.
The pillaged house of Lanercost lies ruined and defaced;
The doers of such sacrilege must cruel vengeance taste.
Let irons fire and famine now scourge the wicked race,
With whom henceforth nor fame nor faith nor treaty can have place.
The Scottish nation, basely led, hath fallen in the dust;
In those who forfeit every pledge let no man put his trust

It is perhaps unfortunate that the Scottish invasion of 1297, an episode that gives us more information on Wallace's career than any other part of

Lanercost Priory. Much damage was inflicted here as Wallace's raiding party moved into Cumberland. No doubt the priory suffered partly as a result of the lack of success of the Scots at the siege of Carlisle 10 miles to the west of Lanercost.

his life, does not show him in the best of lights. An incident recorded in the *Guisborough Chronicle*, however, shows the difficulties he had in preventing his troops from plundering, and also the respect he had for the Church:

> The Scots came to Hexham Priory . . . some Scots spearmen broke in there, shaking their weapons and shouting, 'Bring out the treasures of your church or we'll kill you at once' . . . At that moment William Wallace himself entered, and abusively ordered his men to get out: then he requested the canons to celebrate a Mass, and straightway they began to do so. After the elevation of the Host, Wallace left the church to remove his armour, while the priest made ready to distribute the bread and wine, with the Scots soldiers crowding round him in hopes of stealing the chalice. Indeed when he returned from washing his hands in the sacristy, he found that not only the chalice but all the ornaments of the altar had been pilfered . . . so that he could not finish the Mass he had begun, because everything had been stolen. And while he stood wondering what to do, Wallace

returned, saw what had happened, and told his followers to pursue the men who had done that sacrilege and hang them: but of course they were never found, for the soldiers only pretended to seek them . . . before he left Wallace gave them his letters of protection . . .

The Scottish invasion of northern England in 1297 was in many ways an unsavoury affair showing all the savagery and destructiveness of war. Tax records, rather more independent than the biased and sometimes lurid chronicle accounts, tend to corroborate the references to destruction along the Scottish invasion route. They record particular areas of ruination through evidence of sharply declining tax revenues, for example, in the parishes of north-east Northumberland. There were particularly heavy attacks around the Cheviot Hills and Alnwick seems to have suffered, perhaps as a result of the unexpected assaults on the Scots from men from the castle. There was also a great deal of activity in Tynedale where Bywell and Corbridge were laid waste. John of Fordun gives a terse description of Wallace's progress in Cumberland: '. . . after having burnt up the whole land of Allerdale, and carried off some plunder, he and his men went back safe and sound'. This seems to be supported by tax records: fourteen parishes in the diocese of Carlisle were exempted from the triennial crusading tenth of 1301 because of war damage four years earlier.

Wallace's invasion of Northumberland and Cumberland, 1297.

Bywell Castle on the River Tyne. Wallace's army caused much destruction in Tynedale and Bywell and Corbridge were laid waste.

At the end of 1297 and the beginning of 1298, William Wallace's reputation stood at its highest. His military and political success can be judged partly by the bitterness of English invective against him. The *Song on the Scottish Wars* portrays a particularly stark image of him:

> Now the malignant people return to Scotland; and the honour of knighthood is given to William; from a robber he becomes a knight, just as a swan is made out of a raven, an unworthy man takes the seat when a worthy man is not by . . .

However, the English could not yet take away from William Wallace the position he had earned by early 1298, as recorded in the Charter of William Wallace to Alexander Scrymgeour:

> William Wallace, knight, Guardian of the kingdom of Scotland and commander of its army, in the name of the famous prince the lord, John, by God's grace illustrious king of Scotland, by consent of the community of that realm.

5

WALLACE, GOVERNOR OF SCOTLAND

When Edward I's expeditionary force sailed to Flanders on 24 August 1297, the English King did not anticipate a military disaster such as that which occurred at Stirling Bridge on 11 September. Despite worrying messages, in early August, from Hugh Cressingham that 'peace on the other side of the Scottish sea is still in obscurity', and English administrative control over wide areas of Scotland was poor, Edward I did not feel that the Scots posed a threat. He had, after all, been told in early August that 'your enemies of Scotland were dispersed and frightened from their foolish enterprise' (letter of Hugh Cressingham to Edward I, 4 August 1297) and seems to have believed that the only danger to him came from Stewart, Wishart and Bruce and that this had ended at Irvine. Wishart had, in August, written to Hugh Cressingham apologising for his conduct. Edward, no doubt, still had confidence in the Comyns being able to re-exert their influence over Scottish rebels. The safe conduct, to come to visit his father, issued to Andrew Moray, the younger, on 28 August (four days after Edward's departure to Flanders) was another sign that the English King felt that he had the means to control Scottish nobles (and therefore Scotland) – Andrew's father was still detained in the Tower of London. Edward certainly did not consider that Wallace was a major threat.

Edward's complacency was dispelled after he heard about Stirling Bridge, sometime before 24 September, when he ordered Robert Clifford and Brian Fitz Alan to join forces with the Earl of Warenne and proceed towards Scotland. Walter Bower reports that:

> King Edward, ablaze with mad anger and unable to contain himself through sorrow ... wrote a threatening letter to William the guardian of Scotland, stating among other matters that if the king himself had remained in his kingdom, Wallace would not have dared to attempt such deeds; but if he dared to invade England again, he would at

Caerlaverock Castle. A castle impressive in both strength and style, Caerlaverock with its distinctive red sandstone was at the centre of the Anglo-Scottish war in the early fourteenth century.

once realise that the avenging hands of the king himself were seeking retribution upon him and his men for their presumption. In short, when Wallace heard of the impudence and threatening boasting of the king, he sent a message back to him to say that he would revisit his kingdom once more before the celebration of Easter.

Edward I's anger can well be believed and, no doubt, there was real fear among Englishmen that, in Edward's absence, Wallace would make deep inroads into England. By the fifteenth century, however, Scottish tradition was elaborating on this rumour and in Blind Harry's work Wallace's invasion of England reached St Albans. The reality was that, after the plunder raid on Northumberland, William Wallace's priority was defence against an English counter-attack. An English force under Warenne did, in fact, re-take Berwick and relieve the siege at Roxburgh Castle in early 1298. The *Lanercost Chronicle* gives a good impression of Wallace's strategy at this time, of making supplies for English forces very scarce in southern Scotland:

> . . . after the earls had left Roxburgh, the Scots came by night and burnt the town, and so they did to the town of Haddington, as well as to nearly all the chief towns on this side of the Scottish sea [Firth of Forth], so that the English should find no place of refuge in Scotland. Thus the army of England was soon compelled to return to England through lack of provender.

Perhaps, the plunder raids on Northumberland and Cumberland of October–November 1297 served a dual purpose – the Scots increased their own supplies and, at the same time, deprived any English army approaching Scotland. It was, in effect, a 'scorched-earth' policy, which made it difficult for the English in northern England as well as southern Scotland to obtain provisions.

It was not, however, only a lack of rations that halted English military operations in early 1298. Edward I, in fact, ordered these to cease until he could, personally, take charge of them. The King did not arrive in England until 14 March. He ordered a council, or special conference, to take place in April at York where the campaign would be discussed. The movement of the exchequer from London to York indicated that York would be his military and political headquarters for the Scottish campaign. Edward's summons to the council included the Scottish lords – if they did not appear, they would be considered enemies. Edward himself set off for York in late April, visiting shrines of saints on the way. He was at Ely from 6–7 May, at Bury St Edmunds from 9–10 May and proceeded to Walsingham, Lincoln and Beverley, finally reaching York on 24 May. His army was ordered to muster at Roxburgh, his knights on 23 June and the infantry on 25 June.

Overleaf, background image:
Solway Firth, near Caerlaverock.

YORK AS A WAR CAPITAL

The city wall of York. The late thirteenth and early fourteenth centuries saw the city defences (a circuit of 2 miles) strengthened with stone walls and numerous towers.

Blind Harry's *The Wallace*, followed by the film *Braveheart*, falsely claimed that William Wallace penetrated Yorkshire and even captured York. It is true, however, that Wallace had a dramatic and significant long-term influence on York. Edward I reacted to Wallace's victory at Stirling Bridge on 11 September 1297 by establishing York as his war capital in the summer of 1298. Despite his victory at Falkirk in July 1298, the English King was unable to consolidate control within Scotland and York therefore remained his military and administrative capital between 1298 and 1305, with the

Exchequer, Chancery and the main judicial benches being based there. The resulting influx of officials, lawyers and suitors at the various courts, as well as soldiers, greatly increased the prosperity of the city. The catering profession certainly flourished, as did the trades associated with warfare, such as swordmakers, fletchers, armourers, bowyers and saddlers. However, there were also problems caused by local tradesmen and landlords giving in to the temptations of

Walmgate Bar. The outer defences, the barbican, still remain at Walmgate, though they are no longer to be seen at York's other medieval gateways. The barbicans reflect the ever-growing need for fortifications at York in the century after the Battle of Stirling Bridge.

St Mary's Abbey. When York became a war capital for the English government in 1298 York's finest medieval buildings, such as St Mary's Abbey and Clifford's Tower, were used to house the royal household and government departments. The abbey became home to the Chancery.

The Undercroft at St Leonard's Hospital. The ruins in the Museum Gardens, York, are few but the Undercroft does give a clue that St Leonard's Hospital was one of the largest and finest buildings in medieval York and the largest medieval hospital in England.

profiteering. As a result, in 1301, a series of ordinances were produced; 'No bread over six days is to be sold', 'Taverners, wine sellers and sauce-makers shall not keep bad or putrid wine or vinegar in their houses', 'No doctor is to exercise his profession unless he has been instructed in the art of surgery', 'No-one shall keep pigs which go in the streets by day and night, nor shall any prostitute stay in the city', 'No-one is to put out excrement or other filth or animal manure in the city'. Being a war capital created problems as well as benefits. What is not usually appreciated is how far William Wallace was the catalyst for York's development as a war capital in the Middle Ages.

The cessation of hostilities in the English campaign in early 1298 did, of course, give Wallace a useful and unexpected respite in which to prepare more fully for Edward's army. According to the *Lanercost Chronicle* the Scots:

> . . . set themselves down before the castles of Scotland which were held by the English, to besiege them with all their force, and through famine in the castles they obtained possession of them all, except Roxburgh, Edinburgh, Stirling and Berwick, and a few others; and when they had promised to the English conditions of life and limb and safe conduct to their own land on surrendering the castles, William Wallace did not keep faith with them.

Airth Castle, Falkirk. According to Blind Harry, Wallace's uncle from Dunipace had been captured during the warfare and imprisoned at Airth before being rescued by Wallace. The historical Wallace and his army did not have the expertise to storm castles.

This extract again hints that Wallace did not fight by the normal rules of chivalry. However, there is little contemporary administrative record to show how Wallace prepared his forces. On 29 March, at Torphichen (West Lothian) Wallace granted to Alexander Scrymgeour (in the Charter of William Wallace to Alexander Scrymgeour, 29 March 1298)

> . . . six marks of land in the territory of Dundee . . . and also the constabulary of the castle of Dundee . . . for faithful service and

The church at Airth, now in a severe state of decay, would have been in existence in William Wallace's time but only Blind Harry connects Wallace with this place.

succour given to the said kingdom, in carrying the royal banner in the army of Scotland . . .

This indicates that he was certainly making military appointments. John of Fordun, the most contemporary Scottish source, unfortunately says little about Wallace's organisation of his army but does emphasise his forcefulness in asserting his authority over both the nobility and the burgesses of Dundee. The *Scotichronicon* of Walter Bower and *Chronicle of Pluscarden*, however, have lengthy passages on Wallace's marshalling of the infantry:

Torpichen, West Lothian. William Wallace wrote a letter from here in March 1298. In it he granted the Constabulary of Dundee Castle to Alexander Scrymgeour. Edward I stayed at Torpichen after the Battle of Falkirk.

. . . he encouraged his comrades in arms towards the achievement of whatever plan he had in hand to approach battle for the liberty of their homeland with one mind. And as regards the whole multitude of his followers he decreed on pain of death that once the lesser men among the middling people (or in practice those who were less robust) had been assembled before him, one man was always to be chosen out of five from all the groups of five to be over the other four and called a quaternion; his commands were to be obeyed by them in all matters, and whoever did not obey was to be killed. In a similar manner also on moving up to the men who were more robust and effective there was always to be a tenth man [called a decurion] over each nine, and a twentieth over each nineteen, and so on moving up to each thousand [called a chiliarch] and beyond else to the top . . . With everyone harmoniously approving this law (or substitute for law) they chose him as their captain.

The *Chronicle of Pluscarden* added that this was the advice given to Moses by Jethro. These chroniclers' descriptions of Wallace's fearsome discipline may not be exaggerated but the military system they outline seems to be derived from classical literature rather than William Wallace's own military handbook of 1297. Walter Bower further reports in the *Scotichronicon* how:

. . . from every sheriffdom and shire, barony and lordship, town and village and country estate he had special lists drawn up containing the names of the men between sixteen and sixty who were fit for warfare. So that not one man could be absent unnoticed from a stated time and place without his knowledge, he laid it down as a fundamental law that not only in every barony but also in every sizeable township a gallows was to be erected on which were to be hanged all those inventing excuses to avoid the army when summoned without reasonable cause.

This is, perhaps, more in keeping with the planning Wallace could implement as he waited for Edward I's army.

There was, already, in operation a method of summoning the common army of Scotland. This had been used in 1244 when Alexander II's army briefly confronted Henry III at the border, in 1263 when the Norwegian threat was met at Largs, in 1286 when the Guardians of Scotland were concerned by the threat of civil war and in 1296 when Scotland tried to defeat Edward I's army at Dunbar. Wallace undoubtedly employed this system in his own inimitable and uncompromising way. He could use Parliament to strengthen his military powers – at his trial in 1305 he was accused, among other charges, of convening Scottish parliaments – and, it seems, he had already, before Stirling Bridge, established (with Moray) control over the local administrative structure that was responsible for levying local men for militia duties. With his own undoubted powers of persuasion, William Wallace could ensure that a full complement of the 'common army' would be mustered and, as far as time allowed, trained. The evidence from the Battle of Falkirk was that the Scottish militia was well disciplined and trained.

William Wallace's relationship with the Scottish nobility, and therefore his control over the cavalry element in the Scottish army, has been a controversial question among historians. Scottish nationalist writers of the fourteenth and fifteenth centuries blamed the nobles, and the Comyns in particular, for betraying Wallace at Falkirk. The issue is argued most forcibly by Walter Bower, in the *Scotichronicon*, in the mid-fifteenth century. To him, Scotland under Wallace 'was making a surprising, in fact a successful recovery' until:

> . . . the magnates and powerful men of the kingdom, intoxicated by a stream of envy, seditiously entered a secret plot against the guardian under the guise of expressions of virgin-innocence but with their tails tied together. Hence some who had been restored to their fortresses and domains by him after they had been completely excluded by the same English, muttered with proud hearts and rancorous minds, saying to one another: 'We do not want this man to reign over us.' But the ordinary folk and populace, along with more of the nobles whose attitude was sounder and leaned more towards the public interest, praised the Lord on account of the fact that they themselves, saved from the daring attacks of rivals with the help of such a champion, were able to have the comfort of their own homes. What stubborn folly of fools! Wallace did not force himself into rulership, but by the choice of the estates he was raised up to be ruler after the previously-nominated guardians had been removed. And when you, Scotland, had been headless and unable to defend yourself, Wallace had appeared as a mighty arm and a salvation in time of trouble.

This view and the additional notion, found in John of Fordun, Walter Bower and Wallace's biographer, Blind Harry, that the Comyns were the chief betrayers needs to be set against the background of Scottish nationalist writings of the fourteenth and fifteenth centuries. This context

Overleaf, background image:
Lochmaben Castle.

EDWARD I

Edward I was approaching fifty-seven years of age when William Wallace began his rebellion against English officials in Scotland in the early summer of 1297. Edward had been King of England since 1272, and was not only a very experienced international statesman but still an imposing figure of a man, able to inspire his troops with his stature and physical presence. When his tomb in Westminster Abbey was opened in 1774, his body was seen to be 6 ft 2 in in length, well above average for the time. Edward I was an active international diplomat and mediator in the 1270s and 1280s, keen to use marriage treaties to pursue alliances with the Aragon, the Habsburgs (of Germany) and the Brabant dynasties.

Edward I as a young man and certainly seeming to live up to his nickname 'Longshanks'. (Reproduced by permission of the British Library [Royal MS 2A XX11 f. 219v].)

Holm Cultram Abbey, Cumbria. After Edward I's death at Burgh-on-Sands on 7 July 1307, his body was taken to be buried at Westminster Abbey. However, before the long journey south, Edward's entrails were removed and buried at the Cistercian abbey of Holm Cultram. The English King's chief enemy in 1307, Robert Bruce, also had a connection with the abbey as his father was buried there.

Burgh-on-Sands, where Edward I died. He had already spent some time at Lanercost Priory, having been taken gravely ill as he advanced north to launch a campaign against Robert Bruce. Edward's death is marked by a monument surrounded by iron railings.

Contrary to the image of Edward I as 'Hammer of the Scots' (a phrase to be found on his tomb), his policy towards Scotland was, at first, based on diplomacy. No doubt he gained an insight into Scottish affairs following the marriage of his sister, Margaret, to Alexander III of Scotland at York in 1251. In view of the good social relationships between the royal families of England and Scotland from the 1250s to the 1280s, it was natural, following Alexander III's sudden death in 1286, for Edward to propose a marriage alliance between the very young heiress of Scotland, Margaret, the 'Maid of Norway', and his son, Edward. It was only after 1289 that Edward I took an increasingly interventionist line and seriously underestimated the strength of nationalist feeling in Scotland.

Edward I's Seal, the Great Seal for the Government of Scotland. Reverse: a heater-shaped shield bearing arms, three leopards passant guardant in pale (England). (By permission of the Court of the Lord Lyon.)

was of political instability, the renewed threat of English interference and loss of Scottish independence. Therefore, these writers' review of thirteenth-century politics strongly emphasised the risk posed to the monarchy by faction and lawlessness of the nobility, which in turn threatened Scottish independence. The Comyns were a particular target for blame. It was the politically correct way, in the fourteenth and fifteenth centuries, to paint the Comyns in as black a light as possible in their dealings with Scotland's two nationalist heroes, Wallace and Bruce. Comparisons can be made with the Tudor 'myth' of the Yorkist King Richard III, painted by Shakespeare and others as a crook-backed tyrant. Both 'myths' have been powerful and long lasting.

Historical reality is more complex. The Comyns were officially recognised by Edward I as having returned to the Scottish patriot side by about November/December 1297, though there had been suspicions that they were not working in Edward's interest in August. It is unlikely that they did not support their kinsman, Andrew Moray, as he built up his forces in northern Scotland in the summer of 1297. Noble families such as the Morays, Stewarts, Bruces and the Earl of Lennox took part, with varying degrees of credit, in Scottish resistance in 1297. Stewart and Malcolm, Earl of Lennox, had been involved in the Battle of Stirling Bridge – but only after it had actually been won.

The participation of the nobility in Scottish military resistance is a complicated issue. The patriotic credentials of few – most obviously the Bruces, Patrick, Earl of Dunbar and Gilbert Umphraville, Earl of Angus – could be questioned when hostilities commenced in 1296. It was a war led by the Comyn-dominated aristocratic governing community in the name of King John Balliol fighting for the principles that they had written into the Treaty of Birgham (1290). Yet the nobility did little actual fighting before submitting in 1296 at Dunbar or in 1297 at Irvine, and contributed little to the victory at Stirling Bridge. Their actions suggest that they wanted to use a show of force as a political weapon in negotiations with Edward, knowing that his priority was war against France and hoping that he would prefer a political solution in Scotland, which would with luck preserve their own power and landowning status in the country. Comyns, Stewarts and Bruces all played this diplomatic game of chivalric 'cat-and-mouse'.

On the Scottish side, too, there seemed to be an inbuilt acceptance of the superiority of English military forces, especially the cavalry. Most of the Scottish nobility had social ties with English noble families because of their landholding in England. While this did not make their patriotism any less genuine when peace turned to war, it certainly gave them an understanding of the strengths of English troops. They may well have agreed with the sentiments expressed in the verses of the *Song on the Scottish Wars* written shortly after the Battle of Falkirk:

'Do not be troubled,' said they [the English knights to Edward I] 'if the Scottish thieves sharpen axes for their own heads; one Englishman will slay very many Scots' . . . the English like angels are always conquerors, they are more excellent than the Scotch and Welsh . . .

The Scottish nobility would have been aware that the proportion of knights, i.e. mounted soldiers, to foot soldiers in Scotland was much lower than in England. Matthew Paris, describing the Scottish confrontation with Henry III in 1244, noted that the Scottish had inferior horses to the English. The *Lanercost Chronicle* probably records correctly the relative strengths of the Scottish and English forces at the Battle of Falkirk:

> . . . the Scots gave him battle with all their forces at Falkirk, William Wallace aforesaid being their commander, putting their chief trust, as was the custom, in their foot pikemen, whom they placed in the frontline. But the armoured cavalry of England, which formed the greater part of the army . . .

The question of the loyalty of the Scottish nobility should, therefore, be divided from discussion of the ineffectiveness of the Scottish cavalry.

It is clear that Wallace's association with the Scottish nobility, too, should be separated from the issue of allegiance to the Scottish patriotic cause. Wallace's relationship with his formal overlords, the Stewarts, was ambiguous in the period 1296 to 1298. The English chroniclers' depiction of William Wallace, at the outset, as the frontman of James Stewart and Bishop Wishart and the assumption that Stewart was the mastermind behind Wallace's actions at Stirling Bridge probably represented how they thought Wallace's link with Stewart ought to be rather than the actuality. It is likely that Stewart did encourage Wallace before he (Stewart) came out openly in rebellion with his brother John, Wishart and Robert Bruce in July 1297. However, after the nobles' abject submission, the retainers of most them, including the Stewarts, seem to have accepted Wallace's leadership over that of their own lords. This was evident at Stirling Bridge and this, rather than Stewart's apparent controlling tactics, explains the Stewarts' peripheral role in the battle.

Wallace's relationship with the Bruces has also been the subject of some debate. The Bruces started the war on the English side but the younger Robert Bruce joined the so-called 'aristocratic' revolt in conjunction with his family allies, the Stewarts, and Bishop Wishart. However, it is clear that both as military leader and political leader of Scotland after Stirling Bridge, William Wallace was acting on behalf of King John Balliol. The younger Bruce, and his father, still retained a counter-claim to the Scottish throne and William Wallace must have regarded them with suspicion. At

Wallace Cave by the River Avon. Allegedly, it was in this cave that William Wallace and some of his followers hid in the aftermath of the Battle of Falkirk.

least the Comyn family had always been strong supporters of John Balliol who was, in fact, their kinsman and thus there was common ground with Wallace here. However, while the accusations of treachery against the Comyns at Falkirk may be fourteenth- and fifteenth-century propaganda, there is evidence of tension, even personal animosity, between Wallace and the Comyns.

This ill feeling was openly displayed in 1299 – after Falkirk and after Wallace had ceased to be leader of the political community – at a council meeting at Peebles. David Graham, a front-line Comyn adherent, put forward 'a demand for Sir William Wallace's lands and goods as he was going abroad without leave' (J. Bain [ed.], *Calendar of Documents Relating to Scotland*, II, no. 1978 [Edinburgh, 1881]). Wallace's brother, Malcolm, objected and during the ensuing argument John Comyn, Earl of Buchan, turned on William Lamberton, Bishop of St Andrews, who was clearly defending the Wallaces. The election of Lamberton to the key political and ecclesiastical office of Bishop of St Andrews, on the instruction of William Wallace on 3 November 1297, was probably the real cause of animosity between the Comyns and Wallace. Comyn domination of Scottish politics in the second half of the thirteenth century had been supported by a long line of pro-Comyn bishops of St Andrews – Gamelin (1255–71) had probably been a member of the Comyn family; William Fraser (1279–97) was from a family of Comyn supporters; and it is clear that Master William Comyn, Provost of St Mary's of the Rock at St Andrews (1287–1329) and brother of John Comyn, Earl of Buchan, hoped to follow in this line. The sudden death of William Fraser in France in 1297 and the political vacuum caused by the imprisonment in England of the Comyns and their allies in government from 1296, meant that his candidature could not be pursued by the Comyns during Wallace's political ascendancy. Master William Comyn objected to his exclusion from the election process, Pope Boniface VIII acknowledging that a protest had been made in his letter to William on 7 May 1298. This was, in other words, a 'live' issue in the period leading up to the Battle of Falkirk. This family grievance once again became pertinent in 1299 when William Comyn's brother, John, turned on Lamberton during the baronial council in August 1299. Later, in 1306, it was asserted that William Comyn had, in fact, been elected but superseded by Lamberton.

It was natural for the Comyns, in particular, to feel that their traditional leadership role had been usurped. The Comyns' absence in England in 1296 was also exploited by Bishop Robert Wishart, ally of James Stewart and Wallace, in 1297 – Mr Robert, John Comyn of Badenoch's physician, who had been placed in charge of the church of Great Dalton (Dumfriesshire) 'was unlawfully ousted by the bishop of Glasgow' (Grant G. Simpson and James D. Galbraith [eds], *Calendar of Documents Relating to Scotland*, V, no. 169 [Edinburgh, 1986]). Near contemporary Scottish sources do not attempt to hide Wallace's forthright and uncompromising style and there may have been some truth to a reference in an earlier, more complete text of Walter Bower's *Scotichronicon* that Wallace had suppressed the Comyns in Galloway. Not only were the Comyns politically powerless to appoint their candidate to the bishopric of St Andrews, the nobility in general seemed to have lost their traditional military leadership as a result of their poor showing in 1296 and 1297. They had even lost control over their retainers as Wallace and Moray had shown both before the Battle of Stirling Bridge and during it. The English chroniclers' belief that Wallace was a frontman for James Stewart and Bishop Wishart seems to have less support than John of Fordun's opinion that Wallace:

> . . . in a short time, by force, and by dent of his prowess, brought all the magnates of Scotland under his sway, whether they would or not . . .

The nobility's loss of its traditional leadership in political and military affairs in 1297, together with the forthright manner of Wallace's leadership, were the real causes of tension. It is another matter, however, to talk of Wallace's defeat at Falkirk in terms of betrayal. The battle must be judged on its own merits.

Another seal, perhaps a Privy Seal, of William Lamberton, Bishop of St Andrews (1297–1328). It depicts St Andrew extended on his cross, with a canopy above from which issues a hand placing a crown on his head. At his sides are shields bearing arms. (By permission of the Court of the Lord Lyon.)

There is no doubt that Edward I took the Scottish military threat seriously as he joined his army at Roxburgh in early July 1298. His determination had been clear as soon as he heard news of the English defeat at Stirling Bridge. This extract from the *Song on the Scottish Wars* expresses the tone of his address to his knights: 'Again you must prepare to fight for your country. I would rather conquer once than be often tormented.' On his way north, Edward had visited sacred shrines and collected the banners of northern saints, St John of Beverley and St Cuthbert, to fly at the head of his army. His forces were impressive, strong in armoured cavalry (about 2,500), with an infantry totalling up to 25,000 on the eve of battle and many archers (there were over 10,000 infantry, mainly archers, from Wales, as well as crossbowmen from Gascony) and some 4,000 Irish mercenaries. National fervour had been roused in the English and this was reflected in political songs of the time. The following extract is again from the *Song on the Scottish Wars*:

What does the barbarous brutal and foolish race threaten? Will this perfidy remain unavenged? . . . William Wallace is the leader of these savages . . . 'Do not be troubled', said they (the knights) 'if the

The Upper Tweed valley and Selkirk Forest. Often the route taken by English troops marching on campaign up the east of Scotland, Selkirk Forest was where Wallace acquired a valuable group of archers who fought for him at the Battle of Falkirk.

Overleaf: Eildon Hills, north-west of Dryburgh, where Edward I marched close by during his 1298 campaign.

137

The Cheviot Hills from Chillingham. In his 1298 campaign Chillingham was on Edward I's outward and return routes.

Scottish thieves sharpen axes for their own heads; one Englishman will slay many Scots. It is not the part of a man who has a beard to join mice to a little cart' – Wallace, or Gilmaurus, is scarcely better than a mouse, to whose victory the laurel will never grow; for they want strength and treasure: a bull who has lost his horns is the more eager for the war . . .

Despite such vehement feelings, there must have been some doubt about the loyalty of the very large Welsh contingent.

The enthusiasm of the English and the allegiance of the Welsh would soon be tested as Edward I's army marched north through Lauderdale to Braid, just south of Edinburgh, then on to Kirkliston, just west of Edinburgh. The detailed reporting of the Guisborough chronicler, probably based on an eyewitness account, describes the very real problems Edward I's army faced owing to lack of provisions. Supplies to be brought by ship had been held back by unfavourable winds, and no food could be found in southern Scotland partly because of the famine of the previous year and partly as a result of the deliberate burning and wasting policy of Wallace.

Edward I sent a detachment of troops under Anthony Bek, Bishop of Durham, to try to capture the newly built and Scottish-held Dirleton Castle (with two other neighbouring castles). They had no siege weapons and, as the Guisborough chronicler testified, they were too weak from

Lammermuir Hills. Edward I's campaigns in 1298, 1301 and 1303 passed by these hills up the eastern side of Scotland.

hunger to fight: 'they had to subsist on nothing but a few peas and beans dug out of field'. The King was angry that Bek was unable to carry out his mission but the arrival of some food ships, and Edward I's curt response to Bek's initial failure, led to renewed English attempts to capture the castles and ultimate success within a few days. In the meantime, hunger among the vast infantry army had reached such an advanced stage that some Welshmen were dying. The arrival of a solitary supply ship, laden with wine rather than corn, made the situation worse. Edward I's decision to allow the Welsh to be given wine to bolster their morale backfired when the Welsh became drunk and began brawling, which resulted in a number of priests being killed. English knights were ordered to charge them to restore order. However, the decision to have so many Welshmen in the infantry seemed to be unsound as the Welsh withdrew from the fracas, threatening to join the Scots. Edward's response, 'Who cares if all our enemies join together? With God's help we shall then defeat the whole lot of them in one go', seems to confirm, once more, a dangerous English superiority complex, so often reflected in the popular political songs of the day.

It seemed as if Edward had decided to withdraw to Edinburgh to await the arrival of further supplies when the pro-English Patrick, Earl of

Dirleton Castle. Standing on a rock in an attractive village, this thirteenth-century castle (newly built in 1298) was captured by the English prior to the Battle of Falkirk.

Dunbar, and Gilbert Umphraville, Earl of Angus, brought him a spy whose report changed the English King's mind:

'The Scots army and all your enemies are no more than 18 miles away from here, just outside Falkirk . . . [in Callendar Wood]. They have heard that you intend to retreat to Edinburgh, and they mean to follow you and attack your camp tomorrow night, or at least to fall on your rearguard and plunder your baggage.' Then the King cried: 'May God be praised, for He has solved all my problems. The Scots will have no need to follow me, for I will march to meet them at once.'

This account indicates that the English, up to that stage, had completely lost contact with the Scots and that Edward, without sufficient rations to feed his vast army, had no other option but to retreat to Edinburgh. This also suggests that Wallace's tactic of wasting large areas of southern Scotland had succeeded – attacking the rearguard of a demoralised, hungry enemy was preferable, for Wallace, to engaging in a traditional battle, which favoured Edward's army. Edward, encouraged by the spy's statement, ordered his troops to arm and march towards Falkirk. They camped just east of Linlithgow. In a campaign that had not, up to this point, run smoothly, a further mishap occurred when the King was

A hill at Cockleroy overlooking Linlithgow. Traditionally, it is claimed that Wallace watched Edward I's forces from here as they made camp on their way to meet Wallace's army at Falkirk. The gap between the two summits of Cockleroy is known as Wallace's Cradle.

Overleaf: Linlithgow Castle. Edward I's marches into Scotland (in 1291, 1296, 1298, 1301 and 1303) usually took him to Linlithgow, and just outside here the English army prepared for the Battle of Falkirk.

injured (some chronicles report that he broke two ribs) by his own charger when the animal kicked him as he slept.

William Wallace now seems to have decided to fight a pitched battle, clearly not his favourite option, to remove the English from Scotland. Historians, with hindsight, have criticised Wallace for not continuing with a 'scorched-earth' policy backed with ambush raids but he could not have known that ultimate victory could be achieved this way. Wallace must have been buoyed up by the success at Stirling Bridge, although this was not a typical engagement (despite the way it was portrayed in the film *Braveheart*, i.e. without the bridge).

Wallace prepared a defensive formation to try to counter Edward's massive cavalry superiority. The *Guisborough Chronicle* gives a very detailed account of Wallace's grouping. Callendar Wood was at the rear of his forces, the Westquarter Burn running in front and below him. His infantry troops were positioned 'on hard ground on one side of a hill beside Falkirk'. The English cavalry would be impeded a little by boggy ground before they reached the Scots. Wallace organised his 'army of Scotland' into four great schiltroms described by the Guisborough chronicler as being:

> . . . made up entirely of spearmen, standing shoulder to shoulder in deep ranks and facing towards the circumference of the circle, with their spears slanting outwards at an oblique angle.

These 'shield-rings', bristling with 12-in iron-tipped spears and perhaps comprising between 1,000 and 2,000 men in each schiltrom, must have appeared like huge hedgehogs or porcupines. For further protection, according to the *Rishanger Chronicle*, there were, around each schiltrom,

> . . . a great number of long stakes fixed into the ground and tied together with cords and ropes like a fence so that they would obstruct the passage of the English.

These enclosures must have looked like rings and, before the battle commenced, contemporary English chroniclers recorded Wallace making a typical down-to-earth joke about this: 'I have browght yowe to the rynge, hoppe yef ye kunne [I have brought you to the ring, now dance if you can]' (*Rishanger Chronicle*). Between the schiltroms was Wallace's small body of archers from Selkirk Forest. These were under the command of John Stewart of Jedburgh, brother of James Stewart. At the rear was a small cavalry force contributed by the Scottish nobility, probably including the Comyns, James Stewart, Macduff of Fife, the earls of Lennox, Atholl, Menteith and Strathearn. It is not known whether Robert Bruce was present. The mounted troops were not apparently within the defensive formation and it had been usual practice for the Scots army to be, in effect, two forces, the cavalry of the nobility separated from the 'common army' of infantry, with little coordination between the two as a consequence.

On the morning of 22 July, Edward preferred to pause while his army replenished themselves – most had not eaten for 24 hours – but his main commanders, the earls of Norfolk, Hereford and Lincoln, insisted that a delay would be dangerous because of the closeness of the Scottish forces:

> Then at once, the earls who commanded the vanguard led their men forward in line, for they did not realise at first that a peaty bog lay between them and the enemy: but when they saw this, they directed their men round the west of it, and so were a little delayed. Meanwhile, the second division, under Bishop Bek of Durham and thirty six chosen knights, swung round the bog to the east, making as much speed as possible so as to be first into battle . . . they pressed on and attacked the first Scottish schiltrom, while the earls charged with the vanguard on the other side of the field. The Scots cavalry fled without striking a blow the moment our men appeared, though a few of their lords remained to command the spearmen . . . [while Sir John Stewart] dismounted from his horse and stood in the midst of his people until both he and they – men of noble form and great stature – were all cut down.

The grave of John Stewart in Falkirk churchyard. The tomb of John Graham is also to be found here, another Wallace supporter. Both men lost their lives at the Battle of Falkirk.

Scottish sources concentrate on the key moment in the Scottish defeat and emphasise the flight of the Scottish cavalry as betrayal. John of Fordun states:

> For on account of the ill-will, begotten of the spring of envy, which the Comyns had conceived towards the said William, they, with their accomplices, forsook the field and escaped unhurt.

However, the Scottish horsemen were more suited to harrying, ambushes and skirmishes with foot soldiers and had little chance against a far superior English cavalry force in pitched battle. This had been shown at Dunbar in 1296 and Irvine in 1297. The Scottish cavalry had little role in the victory over the English at Stirling Bridge.

English chroniclers acknowledge that the Scots placed their 'front pikemen . . . in the first line . . . stood their ground and fought manfully' (*Lanercost Chronicle*). The English cavalry had no difficulty

The Wallacestone Monument. Overlooking Falkirk, this 10-ft memorial was erected in 1810 to 'that celebrated Scottish hero Sir William Wallace'.

Lowther Hills. This area was close to the route of Edward I's 1298 campaign between Ayr and Lochmaben.

mowing down the Scottish archers, no doubt killing their leader, John Stewart, but could not penetrate the tightly packed schiltroms. Although few English knights were killed at Falkirk – the most significant casualty being Brother Brian le Jay, Master of the English Templars – over a hundred horses died. The impasse was broken when the English knights were withdrawn and the large number of archers on the English side were ordered to fire into the isolated 'shield-rings' of the Scottish infantry. This was a time when the Scottish cavalry could have given some protection by attacking the archers and thus disrupting the constant flow of arrows. Gradually, the schiltroms, whose spears, according to the Guisborough chronicler, 'were as impenetrable as the branches of a thick wood' to English knights, were themselves pierced by an unbroken bombardment of arrows. As soon as large gaps appeared the English horsemen were ordered to charge and the 'shield rings' were broken. John of Fordun describes the key role played by a detachment of cavalry under Anthony Bek, which went

> . . . by a long road round a hill and attacked the Scots in the rear and thus these, who had stood invincible and impenetrable in front, were craftily overcome in the rear.

Fordun states that Robert Bruce, the future King, was in this English unit, but this seems to be a mistake and must surely refer to Bruce's father, who

The site of Tibbers Castle. This stronghold was taken by the English in the follow-up to their victory at the Battle of Falkirk, 22 July 1298. After Falkirk, Edward I was at Ayr between 26 August and 1 September and reached Tibbers on 3 September.

Opposite, below: Solway Firth looking towards England. Most of the fighting in the Scottish wars after 1298 took place in the south-west, which made the Solway Firth a key crossing area for English armies.

had been consistently on the English side and was known to be in the English army at Falkirk.

Falkirk was a hard and closely fought English victory, but after the 'shield-rings' were broken the Scottish infantry were massacred in their thousands. Wallace escaped during the battle when he saw that Scottish defeat was inevitable. English exultation was recorded in political songs, such as this extract from the *Lanercost Chronicle*:

Berwick, Dunbar and Falkirk too
Show all that traitor Scots can do
England exalt! thy Prince is peerless,
Where thee he leadeth, follow fearless!

The *Song on the Scottish Wars* puts the blame for the Scottish debacle firmly on William Wallace:

Wallace, thy reputation as a soldier is lost; since thou didst not defend thy people with the sword, it is just thou shouldst now be deprived of dominion. But, in my view, thou wilt always be the ass thou wert formerly: – Thou wilt pass into a lasting proverb; thy kingdom is divided, and cannot stand; thy people now drink of the cup which thou hast prepared . . .

Wallace lost the military and political leadership of Scotland following the English success at Falkirk. Yet the defeat was not as decisive as English propaganda would have led contemporaries to believe. Edward I's army marched north but little was achieved apart from the burning of St Andrews and Perth. Stirling was also burnt but it is possible that this may have been part of Wallace's strategy to deny resources to Edward. Provisioning of his troops remained a problem for the English King as he moved southwards towards Ayr, where Robert Bruce, clearly now on the Scottish side, had burnt down the castle as further impediment to the English. Unlike 1296 after Dunbar, Scottish resistance continued after Falkirk, the Scots holding the country north of the Forth and having pockets of resistance in the south. Edward needed another offensive to consolidate his narrowly won victory at Falkirk. Yet problems with supplies, renewed political opposition and financial difficulties in England meant that Edward I had to abandon immediate plans for another campaign and return south. Neither the Scottish patriot movement nor Wallace had been completely eliminated.

Lochmaben Castle. The stone castle at Lochmaben, where some curtain walls survive to their original height, was the chief base of the Bruces in south-west Scotland. After the Battle of Falkirk, Edward I's forces took Lochmaben 4–5 September 1298, after Bruce had rendered Ayr Castle useless to the English by fire.

6

THE WILDERNESS YEARS – BETRAYAL AND MARTYRDOM

Between the battles at Stirling Bridge and Falkirk William Wallace occupied a central role on the military and political stage and, therefore, in historical record. The period after Falkirk saw Wallace apparently revert to being a peripheral figure. Yet so significant was Wallace's position between 11 September 1297 and 22 July 1298 that, despite few references to him in the sources for the time after Falkirk up to his capture and execution in 1305, he still exerted a powerful influence on both Scottish and English operations in the continuing war.

Wallace lost political power after Falkirk as controversially as he had gained it after Stirling Bridge. It is not clear whether he resigned the office of Guardian or was asked to relinquish it. Fordun blames the treachery of the Comyns at Falkirk for Wallace's voluntary renunciation of his office:

> William Wallace, seeing by these and other strong pieces of evidence, the obvious wickedness of the Comyns and those who were in league with them, chose rather to serve with the crowd, than to be set over them, to their ruin, and the grievous wasting of the people. So, not long after the Battle of Falkirk, at the water of Forth, he, of his own accord, resigned the office and charge which he held, of the Guardian . . .

The strength of the condemnation, of course, reflects the need of nationalist narratives of the fourteenth century to condemn the Comyns specifically as rivals and enemies of their heroes, William Wallace and Robert Bruce. The *Lanercost Chronicle* blames the inadequacy of the Scottish cavalry in general rather than the military role of the Comyns in particular: 'all the Scottish cavalry being quickly put to flight'. The accusation of perfidy sits slightly strangely with the Comyns long-held support both of the customs and liberties of Scotland and John Balliol's

kingship (to which William Wallace also keenly adhered). It is also at odds with John of Fordun's own statements that the ruling class accepted John Comyn, the younger, as Guardian of Scotland 'in the same year' as Wallace's resignation 'not long after' Falkirk. Wallace's political leadership of Scotland, his martial Guardianship, could only last as long as he was militarily successful. It is probable, therefore, that he was forced to give up the Guardianship shortly after Falkirk as John Comyn, the younger, and Robert Bruce, Earl of Carrick (and future King), were officially designated joint Guardians by December 1298, in an attempt to establish a new Scottish government of national unity.

Selkirk above St Mary's Loch. This area was often used as a refuge and base in Wallace's 'career' as a fugitive.

Overleaf, background image: Loch Dochart.

ROBERT BRUCE

Robert Bruce's Grave, Dunfermline Abbey. During alterations to the church in 1819, Bruce's remains were found wrapped in a cloth-of-gold shroud. The report of the find noted that the skeleton was of a man between 5 ft 11 in and 6 ft tall.

History is written by the winners rather than the losers. Thus Robert Bruce became the hero of fourteenth- and fifteenth-century Scottish nationalist writers such as John of Fordun, Andrew Wyntoun, Walter Bower and John Barbour. It should be remembered, however, that Robert Bruce's elevation to national hero came after he had defeated Scottish opposition to his 1306 'coup' and had assumed the Scottish kingship. Bruce's standing was secure in Scotland, at least, by 1309 but it was not until his victory over Edward II at the Battle of Bannockburn in 1314 that his position as King of Scotland was truly safe. Fourteenth- and fifteenth-century writers regarded the Battle of Bannockburn as a fitting climax of a just, indeed a holy, war, as expressed by John of Fordun in *The Chronicle of the Scots Nation* (*c.* 1380):

But God in His mercy, as is the wont of His fatherly goodness, had compassion . . .; so He raised up a saviour and champion unto them . . . Robert Bruce. The man . . . putting forth his hand unto force, underwent the countless and unbearable toils of the heat of the day . . . for the sake of freeing his brethren . . .

Bruce's heart stone, Melrose Abbey. Robert Bruce made a deathbed wish for his heart to be buried at the abbey after it was taken on Crusade by James Douglas. It lay buried there until discovered by archaeologists in the 1920s. It was re-found in 1996 (the burial spot was not indicated in the 1920s) and returned in 1998 with the present stone marking the heart's re-burial for the third time in its history.

A NOBLE HART MAY HAVE NANE EASE

GIF FREEDOM FAILYE

The Robert Bruce Statue, Bannockburn. The Pilkington Jackson bronze monument, modelled on the equestrian representation on the King's Second Great Seal, was unveiled by HM Queen Elizabeth II on 24 June 1964 to celebrate the 650th anniversary of the Battle of Bannockburn.

Yet in the context of William Wallace, Bruce's achievement and his status as a winner came after Wallace's death in 1305. Robert Bruce was twenty-two years old in 1297 when William Wallace emerged 'from his den' and his actions between 1297 and 1305 show uncertainty about how to achieve his family's dynastic ambitions in Scotland. This contrasts with William Wallace's undaunted and single-minded approach in these years – Bruce's boldness and certainty would come in 1306.

The site of Castle Doon, Loch Doon. The Bruce earldom of Carrick had Turnberry Castle, Ayrshire, as its headquarters. The castle at Loch Doon also had great strategic significance and, until damming in the 1950s, it could be seen on an island in the loch.

That William Wallace left the highest office in Scotland in anger is reflected in an English spy's report (see J. Bain [ed.], *Calendar of Documents Relating to Scotland*, II, no. 1978 [Edinburgh, 1881]) of an argument that broke out at the baronial council in Peebles in August 1299:

> At the council sir David Graham demanded the lands and goods of sir William Wallace because he was leaving the kingdom without the leave or approval of the guardians. And sir Malcolm, sir William's brother, answered that neither his lands nor his goods should be given away, for they were protected by the peace in which Wallace had left the kingdom, since he was leaving to work for the good of the country . . .

It seems that, after the Battle of Falkirk, Wallace was once more out of sympathy with the traditional aristocratic leadership but, just as importantly, they no longer had an affinity with him. Present at the council meeting were Malcolm Wallace, William's brother – described by the spy as 'of the earl of Carrick's following', William Lamberton, Bishop of St Andrews, and James Stewart, who tried to act as mediator. A year after Falkirk, William Wallace was, clearly, still a cause of much bitterness in Scottish political circles. While his brother was in Bruce's following, it was unlikely that William Wallace, with his strong defence of John Balliol's kingship, would be anything other than suspicious of the motives of Robert Bruce, who was in the unlikely position of acting in 1298 and 1299 on behalf of Balliol. James Stewart's actions in 1299, too, appear not to be those of a firm supporter of William Wallace's cause. It is hardly surprising, given the nature of the new government in Scotland, that William Wallace, as he had done in the past, acted in 1298 independently 'without the leave or approval of the guardians'. The impression given by the account of the 1299 council is that the political community, having been bullied by his uncompromising manner into supporting his military leadership, was taking the opportunity of putting Wallace in his proper place. Wallace would not serve under their terms. John of Fordun may have been correct in his comment that Wallace 'chose rather to serve with the crowd'.

The reality of hard political in-fighting in Scotland after Falkirk should be set against the rather charged nationalist writings of Walter Bower and Blind Harry in the fifteenth century. To them Wallace's main legacy after Falkirk was the kindling of a true vocation of nationalism in Robert Bruce, the future King. Bower was not content simply to repeat Fordun's inaccurate report that Robert Bruce (mistaken in probability for his father) played a significant role in the English victory at Falkirk. Instead, he told an elaborate story linking Wallace and Bruce with a mutually held cause:

Pursuing them [Wallace and his men] from the other side, Robert de Bruce . . . is said to have called out loudly to William, asking him who it was that drove him to such arrogance as to seek so rashly to fight in opposition to the exalted power of the king of England and the more powerful section of Scotland. It is said that William replied like this to him: 'Robert, Robert, it is your inactivity and womanish cowardice that spur me to set authority free in your native land . . .'

On account of all of this Robert himself was like one awakening from a deep sleep, the power of Wallace's words so entered his heart that he no longer had any thought of favouring the views of the English. Hence, as he became every day braver than he had been, he kept all these words uttered by his faithful friend, considering them in his heart . . .

This powerful picture, which supports the traditional view that Robert Bruce took over the leadership of the national cause after Wallace's capture and execution in 1305, is far from the reality of 1298. Robert Bruce, the younger, if not at Falkirk in 1298, was certainly on the Scottish side at the time – shortly after Falkirk he seems to have been at Ayr setting fire to the castle in order to prevent its use by the English. In 1298 Wallace and Bruce probably regarded each other with mutual suspicion. At this time Bruce was just breaking into the political elite in Scotland, and his opinion of Wallace was likely to have been shared by other aristocratic families. Wallace must have been aware that the Scottish 'cause' that he was fighting for, i.e. Scottish independence under King John Balliol, was at odds with the Bruces' ambition to found their own dynasty. Robert Bruce, the future King, started the war of 1296 on the English side opposing a Scottish government trying to uphold John Balliol's kingship and Scottish independence. Despite the apparent confluence of interests in 1297 and 1298 when the young Robert Bruce came over to the 'patriot' side, the actions of Robert Bruce between 1298 and 1305 do not support Bower's story that Bruce became a true patriot in Wallace's image after 1298.

It seems that William Wallace left Scotland without the leave or approval of the Guardians (both Bruce and Comyn) to assist in the diplomatic negotiations in France and at the papacy on behalf of Scotland. As a military man, he had observed the weaknesses of the Scottish in the face of the English cavalry, and would, no doubt, have been looking for French military help as part of the Scots–French alliance of 1295. In addition, he would, of course, have been interested in pursuing all avenues to secure the release of King John Balliol. It is not known when Wallace left Scotland, although he was present at the French court by November 1299. It is unlikely that he left Scotland before being briefed by William Lamberton, who owed his elevation to the bishopric of St Andrews to

Overleaf: Dumbarton Castle, a naturally strong site similar in origin to the great rocks at the castles of Edinburgh and Stirling. Dumbarton rises dramatically from the north shore of the Clyde as it meets the River Leven, where Wallace was held after his capture. Most of the medieval stronghold has been destroyed by later fortifications, though some sections of the medieval curtain wall and the portcullis arch remain.

Wallace. Lamberton was consecrated in Rome on 1 June 1298, before joining fellow Scots at the French court. It should be remembered that Lamberton's predecessor, William Fraser, had died in France in 1297, no doubt, also, on an ambassadorial mission. Scottish representatives at the French court, in 1298, seem to have included Bishop Matthew Crambeth of Dunkeld, John Soules and the Abbot of Melrose. This Scottish diplomatic endeavour seems to have had some success judging by the letters of Philip IV, King of France, and Pope Boniface VIII, in June and July 1298, to Edward I demanding the liberation of John Balliol. Although this request was at first refused, Balliol was released into papal custody in July 1299. The Pope also wrote to Edward I urging the English King to abandon the war in Scotland. Boniface claimed that

> . . . from ancient times the realm of Scotland belonged rightfully, and is known still to belong to the Roman church . . . you are known to have safeguarded the interests of the nobles . . . by writing [in the Treaty of Birgham, 1290] that the realm should remain for ever entirely free, and subject, or submitted to nobody.

Scotland was constantly strengthening its diplomatic mission in France, the Abbot of Jedburgh and John Wishart being warmly received in April 1299. Discussion of the nature of French aid to the Scottish cause was clearly at the heart of the negotiations which Lamberton had been leading on behalf of the Scottish mission. Apparently Lamberton had unsuccessfully proposed to Philip IV that the French King's brother, Charles of Valois, should be sent to Scotland with an army. It seems probable that Lamberton would have briefed Wallace thoroughly on these matters when he returned to Scotland, which he had done by August 1299. Given Wallace's expertise in martial affairs, it would have seemed perfectly natural for him to volunteer his services to press the French King further on the military needs of France's ally, Scotland. Wallace had left for France by 19 August (the date of the baronial council in Peebles where discussion of Wallace's lands led to an ugly brawl between Comyn and Bruce supporters) and in early August did not take part with the rest of the Scottish leaders in an extensive raid across Scotland, south of the Forth. By November 1299, Wallace and a small group of associates (Roger Mowbray, William Vieuxpont, Richard Fraser, Edmund Leilholm and Hugh Fotheringay) were at the French court in Paris. All had links with the Balliol cause and it seems that they were formally representing Balliol interests to the French King – perhaps suggesting the restoration of Balliol to Scotland. The fact that they were receiving loans and payments from Philip IV in November 1299 implies that Wallace's party were warmly welcomed at the French court.

The Robroyston Monument.
This cross was erected to
commemorate the capture of
William Wallace at Robroyston.
It was unveiled in 1900.

English sources give a rather less glowing account of Wallace's reception in France. The *Rishanger Chronicle* records that William Wallace and five knights were seized by the King of France on arrival in Amiens; the King of France subsequently offered to deliver Wallace to King Edward. Such an action, if correctly reported, would only have been feasible during a temporary truce between England and France. This, perhaps, could have occurred during the summer of 1299 following the conclusion of the marriage agreement between Philip IV's sister, Margaret, and Edward. Edward's reply to Philip's offer, according to Rishanger, was to ask the French King to hold Wallace in his care in France. This rather puzzling piece of evidence suggests that Edward I no longer felt that Wallace was a threat to him – it would not, of course, be the first time that he underestimated Scottish 'patriot' resistance. By November 1300, the date of the next known reference to William Wallace in France, it is clear that Wallace was well regarded at the French court (after a stay of one year). At this time, Philip IV wrote a letter of recommendation, on Wallace's behalf, to his (French) agents in Rome asking them to help 'our beloved William le Walloys of Scotland knight' in his diplomatic business with the Pope. Fifteenth-century Scottish nationalist writings have elaborated considerably on Wallace's adventures in France. According to a

"DICO·TIBI·VERUM·LIBERTAS·OPTIMA·RERUM
NUNQUAM·SERVILI·SUB·NEXU·VIVITO·FILI"
TAUGHT·TO·WALLACE·IN·HIS·BOYHOOD

✠·THIS·MEMORIAL·ERECTED·1900·A·D·
BY·PUBLIC·SUBSCRIPTION·IS·TO·MARK·THE·SITE
OF·THE·HOUSE·IN·WHICH·THE·HERO·OF·SCOTLAND
WAS·BASELY·BETRAYED·AND·CAPTURED·ABOUT
MIDNIGHT·ON·5ᵀᴴ·AUGUST·1305·WHEN·ALONE·WITH
HIS·FAITHFUL·FRIEND·AND·CO-PATRIOT·KERLIE
WHO·WAS·SLAIN

WALLACE'S·HEROIC·PATRIOTISM
AS·CONSPICUOUS·IN·HIS·DEATH·AS·IN·HIS·LIFE
SO·ROUSED·AND·INSPIRED·HIS·COUNTRY·THAT
WITHIN·NINE·YEARS·OF·HIS·BETRAYAL·THE·WORK
OF·HIS·LIFE·WAS·CROWNED·WITH·VICTORY·AND
SCOTLAND'S·INDEPENDENCE·REGAINED·ON·THE
FIELD·OF·BANNOCKBURN

The plaque on the Robroyston Monument gives details of William Wallace's capture.

later version of Walter Bower's chronicle, Wallace impressed his hosts by fighting French pirates and English invaders in France. Blind Harry develops the same tradition in his own inimitable way, detailing Wallace's struggles not only with the French pirate known as the 'Red Rover' but also an angry French lion!

There are no specific contemporary details about his business at the papal court but it is apparent that Wallace, self-appointed or otherwise, played a key role in putting diplomatic pressure on both the French and papal courts to secure both military aid and the restoration of John Balliol to Scotland. With Balliol's release into the custody of the papacy in July 1299, it was an obvious next step for Wallace to move from the French to the papal court to secure the freedom of John Balliol and counter the diplomatic efforts of the English. Wallace, of course, cannot be given all or even the major credit for the success of the Scottish pleas at the papal court during this period. Master Baldred Bissett probably deserves the most acclaim for the revival of John Balliol's fortunes there. Balliol's reinstatement as King of Scotland seemed a growing possibility in 1301. In the summer of that year he was released from papal custody and, no doubt, with Philip IV's support was returned to his ancestral home at Bailleul-en-Vimeu, in Picardy. The Truce of Asnières, negotiated in France and ratified by King Philip, granted a truce to the Scots in the war with England to last from 26 January to 1 November 1302 but there was no agreement about the future of John Balliol. According to this settlement, the French were to hold certain lands in the south-west of Scotland during the truce.

These developments on the continent had a significant impact on the leadership of the Scottish political community. The years 1298 to 1304 saw many changes in the composition of the Guardianship, the presence of the Comyns being the one constant factor, simply due to their dominant landowning and political power and their network of allies and castles. The tense joint leadership of John Comyn and Robert Bruce in 1298 gave way to a triumvirate in which Bishop Lamberton acted as a stabilising influence. By May 1300, however, Robert Bruce had resigned to be replaced by the pro-Comyn, Ingram Umphraville. This new triumvirate lasted until early 1301 when they were, apparently, superseded by John Soules, appointed by John Balliol directly as his agent in Scotland, pending his return. A number of official documents issued between 10 July 1301 and 23 November 1302 refer either to John Soules acting in the name of (not on behalf of) King John or are royal acts issued by King John himself. There is no doubting his special role in Scotland from 1301 but it is probable that John Soules was acting with Comyn rather than instead of him. He was the representative of Balliol, perhaps nominated as a result of French influence, and seen as the link between Balliol and the Comyn-led Scottish political community. Anyone who wanted to make an impact on Scotland in the 1290s and 1300s had to seek some accommodation with the Comyns because of their landed, political and military power. This was true for John Balliol in 1301, as it had been for Edward I in the 1290s and as it would be for Robert Bruce in 1306. This was also the case for William Wallace but, as has been seen, Wallace was an uncompromising individual.

Fear of the imminent return of John Balliol to Scotland caused Robert Bruce to leave the Scottish patriot side and return to an alliance with Edward I by February 1302 (as quoted in E.L.G. Stones, *Anlgo-Scottish Relations 1174–1328, Some Selected Documents* [Oxford, Clarendon Press, 1970]):

> Because Robert . . . fears that the . . . realm of Scotland might be removed from the hands of the king, which God forbid, and delivered to John Balliol, or to his son, or that the right [landed rights or his claim to the throne?] might be put in question or reversed . . .

However, just as the diplomatic efforts of Wallace and others in Paris seemed set to restore Balliol to Scotland, the French army suffered a devastating defeat at the hands of Flemish forces at Courtrai on 11 July 1302. This meant that Philip IV was forced to concentrate on Flanders

Overleaf: Solway Firth, near Caerlaverock. The Solway Firth was the main crossing into Scotland for Scottish campaigns in the south-west, and for this reason Edward I could not afford the strategically important castle of Caerlaverock to remain in Scottish hands.

rather than Scotland. An Anglo-French peace followed (made on 20 May 1303) which excluded the Scots, who were thus effectively abandoned as allies, despite the intervention of John Soules, William Lamberton, James Stewart and John Comyn, Earl of Buchan, in Paris. It must also have been a bitter blow to William Wallace's diplomatic efforts. Scottish hopes of valuable assistance from the continent were further dashed when Pope Boniface VIII abandoned his support for the Scottish patriot cause in 1302, ordering the bishops of Scotland, in a letter of 13 August, to make every effort to promote peace with Edward I, and accusing Robert Wishart, Bishop of Glasgow, of encouraging Scottish resistance against the English King. The events of 1302, undoubtedly, persuaded William Wallace to return to Scotland and renew his military career fighting the English in Scotland. His work at the French and papal courts between 1299 and 1302 has, because of fragmentary evidence, been underestimated as part of his overall contribution to the patriot causes. It is possible that he also tried to win support from King Hakon V of Norway – when he was captured in 1305 a safe conduct from the Norwegian King was among the documents found on him – and this may explain his absence from record between the Battle of Falkirk and the summer of 1299.

What was the situation in Scotland when William Wallace returned, sometime in late 1302 or early 1303? Edward I had not consolidated his victory at Falkirk with a follow-up campaign in 1299 because of political

Caerlaverock Castle. Caerlaverock was 'in shape like a shield' according to a contemporary ballad about the siege of 1300. Its capture by the English strengthened their position in the south-west.

Siege of Caerlaverock by David Simon. This reconstruction shows that the siege of Caerlaverock was not ended by spectacular assaults of knights but rather by the more mundane work of siege engineers. (Crown copyright: Reproduced courtesy of Historic Scotland.)

problems in England. He was unable to lead a military expedition into southern Scotland until the summer of 1300. Only in the south-east of Scotland was English authority reasonably secure between 1298 and 1303, and most of the fighting took place in the south-west where the English only controlled parts. The Scottish cavalry again took flight at the Cree in August 1300 but, in general, the Scots showed that they had learnt something from Falkirk by adopting more harrying tactics. The Scots mastery of the surrounding countryside enabled them to capture Stirling late in 1299 as a result of the English garrison's lack of provisions. The main achievement of Edward I's 1300 campaign was the capture of Caerlaverock Castle in July of that year. The siege was graphically described in the poem the *Song of Caerlaverock*:

But their courage was considerably lowered during the attack by brother Robert who sent numerous stones from the 'robinet' . . . Moreover, on the other side he was setting up three other very large engines, of great power and very destructive, which cut down and break through whatever they strike . . . nothing is safe from their strokes . . . And when they saw they could not hold out any longer or endure more, they begged for peace and put out a pennon but the man who displayed it was shot through the hand into the face with an arrow by some archer . . . the whole army rejoiced at the news of the capture of the castle which was so noble a prize.

Edward's son largely led the English offensive of 1301. Scottish tactics were the same as the *Lanercost Chronicle* described them in 1300 and consequently little was achieved, '. . . because they [the Scots] always fled before him, skulking in moors and woods.' The English, however, took the important Scottish castles at Bothwell and Turnberry (Bruce's headquarters in Carrick), but supply problems and general lack of progress led to Edward agreeing a truce from 26 January to November 1302. It is possible that Wallace returned to Scotland sometime in late 1302 or early 1303 but not as the Scots 'chief leader and commander', as claimed in the *Rishanger Chronicle*. It is clear that John Comyn, the younger, was sole political and military leader of the Scots from the autumn of 1302. It was in this capacity that he led a Scottish force (along with Simon Fraser) on a successful, surprise raid against the forces of Sir John Segrave at Roslin (south-west of Edinburgh) on 24 February 1303. There is no mention of William Wallace's involvement, though Blind Harry gives Wallace the credit for the victory. This achievement was recognised as a great boost to morale by the Scots in Paris, who wrote to Comyn on 25 May:

For God's sake do not despair . . . it would gladden your hearts if you would know how much your honour has increased in every part of the world as the result of your recent battle with the English.

Lochindorb Castle, Badenoch. This castle was the main base of the Comyn lords of Badenoch, leaders of the political community of Scotland for most of the period of the Scottish wars, 1296–1304. Their importance is attested by Edward I's use of Lochindorb Castle as a base in 1303 to receive the formal submission of northern Scotland.

The Seal of Simon Fraser, c. 1296. Like William Wallace, Fraser resisted joining in the general submission of the Scots in February 1304. He received a similarly harsh punishment to Wallace a year after Wallace's death. (By permission of the Court of the Lord Lyon.)

The letter also expressed a rather naïve belief that the King of France would still look after the interests of the Scots and bring Scotland into the peace agreement. Bishop Lamberton sent a similar letter of encouragement – perhaps written at the same time – to his ally, William Wallace. Lamberton urged Wallace to help the Scottish political community to fight against Edward I. Practical help was offered in the form of revenues from his bishopric, which his officials were ordered to supply to Wallace.

Spurred on by the English defeat at Roslin, Edward I launched the first English campaign against northern Scotland since 1296. It is notable that the offensive targeted Comyn power in Scotland north of the Forth. Edward's route, bypassing the key castle of Stirling (using three floating bridges), took in major centres of Comyn influence in the north – Aberdeen, Banff and the private Comyn castles of Lochindorb (which he used as a base to receive the submission of the north) and Balvenie (Mortlach) – during August and September 1303. There was little resistance as the Scots sought to avoid a pitched battle. It is possible that Wallace was involved in the raid with other Scots (Comyn and Fraser) on Annandale and down to south Cumberland in June 1303 – this may have been a diversionary attack to stretch Edward I's supply lines.

Having returned to Scotland to reinforce military efforts, Wallace must have been disturbed by the steady flow of Scottish support to Edward I.

Selkirk near Happrew. Selkirk Forest again provided cover for William Wallace (with Simon Fraser) in early 1304 when the English forces tried to track him down. He was nearly captured at Happrew, west of Peebles.

The Macdougalls had submitted in 1301, as did Alexander Balliol, Robert Bruce had submitted by early February 1302, Alexander Abernethy also in 1302 and William, Earl of Ross, in September 1303 (when he was released from prison in England). In February 1304, John Comyn, accepted political leader of Scottish resistance, was trying to secure the best terms for those Scots who had not yet surrendered to Edward. He also seemed to be acting for the Scots delegation in France. Again Wallace and Comyn disagreed, fundamentally, on the methods used to preserve the country's independence. Comyn, as ever the pragmatist, sought to negotiate from a position of military strength – the Scottish army had not been defeated in 1303 and had won some status by the victory at Roslin. The preliminary terms of submission set out by Comyn required, in return, that all the laws, usages, customs and franchises should be kept as they were in Alexander III's time. In keeping with his uncompromising approach to the patriot cause (whether by fighting or diplomacy), Wallace decided (along with Simon Fraser) to fight on.

Comyn, acting on behalf of the community of the realm in Scotland, surrendered at Strathord, near Perth, on 9 February 1304, and discussions for a settlement commenced. In late February 1304, Edward, at Dunfermline, dispatched a mounted force under John Segrave, William Latimer and Robert Clifford on a secret mission into Selkirk Forest where Wallace and Simon Fraser were thought to be lurking (J. Bain [ed.], *Calendar of Documents Relating to Scotland*, II, no. 1432 [Edinburgh, 1881]):

> . . . when these officers come to the water of Forth, they are to search strictly their followers, and if they find any strangers, to arrest them with horses and harnesses . . .

This unit did come upon and defeat Fraser and Wallace's forces at Happrew in Stobo, just to the west of Peebles, but the Scots managed to escape. In the English party was Robert Bruce, the future King, who had been active in Edward's service for two years. Despite the failure to capture Wallace, Bruce, Segrave and their soldiers were commended by Edward (J. Bain [ed.], *Calendar of Documents Relating to Scotland*, II, no. 1432 [Edinburgh, 1881]):

> . . . [Edward] applauds their diligence in his affairs, and begs them to complete the business they have begun so well and to bring matters to a close before they leave the parts on that side [the Forth]. He urges them earnestly 'as the cloak is well made, also to make the hood'.

Edward I had failed to consolidate his military victories over the Scots at Dunbar in 1296, Irvine in 1297 and Falkirk in 1298 – he had been unable to eradicate resistance. This fact may have preyed on his mind as he sought to bring a final end to the war in 1304, following another successful military campaign in 1303. This seems to have revealed itself in a harsher attitude towards those who had not submitted to him by February 1304. When Alexander Abernethy (who had surrendered to Edward I in 1302) was, like Bruce and Segrave, trying to track down William Wallace, he enquired how Wallace was to be treated, if taken. Edward I's reply (3 March 1304) is forthright (J. Stevenson [ed.], *Documents Illustrative of the History of Scotland 1286–1306*, II):

And in reply to the matter wherein you have asked us to let you know whether it is our pleasure that you should hold out to William le Waleys any words of peace, know this, that it is not our pleasure by any means that either to him, or to any of his company, you hold out any word of peace, unless they place themselves absolutely and in all things at our will, without any exception whatsoever.

In March 1304, Edward I convened Parliament in Scotland (at St Andrews) at which a declaration of outlawry was passed on those – William Wallace, Simon Fraser and the Stirling garrison – who held out against him. Edward's conduct of the three-month siege (May–July 1304) at Stirling Castle is indicative of his growing desire to make examples of those who defied him. The garrison at Stirling was not allowed to surrender with honour on 20 July but was rather cruelly subjected to some target practice for one of Edward's new siege-weapons, 'the Warwolf'. The following extract is taken from J. Bain, *Calendar of Documents Relating to Scotland*, II, no. 1560:

> Stirling castle was absolutely surrendered to the King . . . without conditions; but the King wills that none of his people enter till it is struck with the 'Warwolf'; and that those within defend themselves from the said 'Wolf' as they best can.

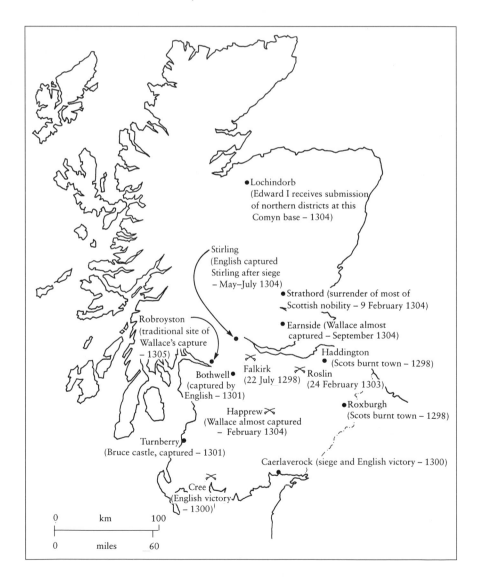

Main events, 1298–1305.

Lindores Abbey, Fife. Wallace's last-known armed conflict took place in September 1304 at Black Earnside (Ironside). This was between Abernethy and Lindores.

The terms agreed in the surrender negotiations, which started in February 1304 and were not finalised until 1305, are a further indication of Edward's desire to punish those who continued to resist him. When Simon Fraser submitted in July 1304, William Wallace became even more the symbol of resistance to Edward. On the day after the siege of Stirling had ended, Edward I ordered John Comyn, Alexander Lindsay, David Graham and Simon Fraser, all with sentences of exile hanging over them at this stage in the surrender negotiations (F. Palgrave [ed.], *Documents and Records Illustrating the History of Scotland* [London, 1837]),

> . . . to make an effort between now and the twentieth day of Christmas 13th January 1305 to take Sire William Wallace and hand him over to the king so that he can see how each one bears himself whereby he can have better regard towards the one who takes him, with regard to exile or ransom or amend of trespass or anything else in which they are obliged to the king.

Edward was stepping up the pressure on Wallace's former 'allies' in the patriot party. He therefore refused to admit James Stewart, John Soules and Ingram de Umphraville to his peace until Wallace was captured. Edward clearly linked Stewart and Bishop Wishart with support for

Earnside (Ironside), site of the last skirmish in which William Wallace is known to have participated (September 1304). In medieval times this was a heavily wooded area, a suitable refuge for a hunted outlaw. Once again Wallace was lucky to escape.

Dumbarton Castle, where Wallace was imprisoned after his arrest at Robroyston. John of Menteith, who took responsibility for his capture and custody, was Sheriff of Dumbarton.

Wallace's activities. In the initial surrender terms of 4 February 1304, Wishart was due to be punished with two or three years' exile from Scotland 'for the great evils he has brought about'. James Stewart's lands were not restored to him until November 1305. Wallace's special place in Scottish resistance was recognised from the outset of the discussions: 'Item about William Wallace, the king intends that he be received to his will and ordinance.' There was to be no compromise regarding the coercion of the leaders of the 'patriot' party, and financial rewards — the man who first discovered Wallace was promised 40 marks, his following would share 60 marks — still did not lead to the arrest of William Wallace in 1304. He was almost apprehended, once again, in a skirmish at Earnside (Lindores, Fife) in September 1304.

William Wallace was eventually betrayed (by whom, it is not known) in 1305. He was captured on 3 August by John of Menteith who, since his submission to Edward I between September 1303 and March 1304, had been entrusted with the sheriffdom of Dumbarton. Although Scottish sources put all the blame for the betrayal on him (and Edward I was keen to reward him with land worth £100), it is not certain whether Menteith was doing any more than fulfilling his duties in the area of his responsibility. As Menteith later appeared in the following of Robert Bruce, it has even been suggested that Robert Bruce could have been

Wallace's Well at Robroyston. There are a number of memorials to Wallace's capture in Robroyston in 1305 in the town. These include a monument and Wallace's Well, though there is nothing to connect Wallace with the latter.

implicated in Wallace's arrest. Bruce undoubtedly would feel that the removal of one of the two mainstays and supporters of John Balliol's kingship – John Soules being the other – could improve the chances of a Bruce claim. Bruce came close, indeed, to taking Wallace himself near Peebles in late February 1304. It seemed rather that the traditional ruling families of Scotland preferred to leave Wallace to his fate. Comyns, Bruces, Stewarts and the bishops of St Andrews and Glasgow were engaged in their own political games – to achieve as much independence for Scotland as they could but at the same time ensure retention of political power in Scotland for themselves. Yet the mystery over the degree of contact and cooperation between the traditional ruling families of Scotland and Wallace in 1297 (when active revolt began) still existed in 1305 (at his capture).

When he was arrested – according to Peter of Langtoft, 'Sir John de Menteith . . . took him in bed beside his strumpet' – documents were found in his possession that included confederations and ordinances made between Wallace and the magnates of Scotland. There were certainly plots afoot in 1304, though it is not known whether Wallace was involved in them. On 11 June 1304, for instance, Robert Bruce made a secret bond with Bishop William Lamberton, promising 'to be of one another's counsel in all their business and affairs at all times and against whichever individuals'. Bruce was clearly seeking wider support even if this meant making unlikely partnerships. Any conspiracy would have to take account of the Comyns' power (still not destroyed after their tactful submission to Edward I in early 1304) and it seems possible that a similar general agreement to an alliance of mutual cooperation may have been made between Robert Bruce and his fierce rival, John Comyn of Badenoch, in 1304. Those responsible for a plot may also have sought military affiliation with William Wallace, whose popular support was known to Scottish and English leaders alike. The involvement of Lamberton (a close ally of Wallace) and Wishart (who had also been associated with Wallace in 1297) in the scheme to help Bruce usurp the Scottish throne suggests that Wallace may have been approached at some stage. It is also probable, given his loyalty to the Balliol cause, that Wallace would have rejected such overtures, as John Comyn did in 1306.

After his arrest, Wallace was sent to London in the custody of John Segrave. He arrived there on 22 August 1305 and was taken to the property of William Leyre, alderman, in the parish of Fenchurch. The intended public humiliation of Wallace started the next morning with a procession through crowds to Westminster Hall with the prisoner being led on horseback. A crown of laurels was placed on his head, a mocking riposte to the popular story that Wallace had once boasted that he would wear a crown at Westminster. There was no trial. Peter Mallory, Justiciar of England, read the indictments against Wallace who, as an outlaw, had no

The Houses of Parliament. After his capture, William Wallace was taken to London and led to Westminster Hall, the oldest part of the Houses of Parliament. One of Wallace's offences was that he had convened parliaments in Scotland.

right to a trial and could only expect judgement and sentence. Wallace was charged with committing 'all the felonies and seditions he possible could' against Edward, killing the Sheriff of Lanark, usurping the power of 'lord superior' of Scotland, convening parliaments, pursuing a policy of alliance with the French; he was also accused of war atrocities – killing, burning, destruction of property and sacrilege. Wallace's only known outburst during his 'trial' was his denial of the charge of treason, 'that he had never been a traitor to the king of England' because he had never acknowledged any allegiance to Edward I.

After John Segrave read the sentence, Wallace had to face the penalty that his crimes warranted; it was not specially devised just for Wallace. The various stages of Wallace's ritual punishments began when he was stripped, bound to a hurdle and dragged behind a horse from Westminster to the Tower, then through the city streets to Aldgate, on to Smithfield where he was hanged, cut down while still alive, disembowelled and then beheaded. According to Matthew of Westminster, his heart and entrails 'from which his perverse plans had arisen' were burnt, and his corpse was hacked into four pieces. His head was hoisted onto London Bridge and his four quarters were displayed at Newcastle upon Tyne, Berwick, Stirling and Perth. Peter Langtoft outlines how Wallace was treated:

> . . . judged on the following conditions: – first to be drawn to the
> gallows for his treasons, – to be hung for robbery and slaughter, –

The Tower of London. The first part of William Wallace's punishment involved being dragged from Westminster to the Tower. Following the English victory at Dunbar in 1296 and John Balliol's submission, Balliol, his chief supporters, Scottish royal regalia and all records were brought to the Tower of London.

Whitehall. Wallace was paraded through the streets of London from Whitehall to the Tower.

Eleanor Statue, Charing Cross. This is one of a number of Eleanor crosses commemorating Edward I's first queen who died in 1290. There is an effigy of Queen Eleanor (by William Torel) on her tomb in Westminster Abbey. Edward I's grief at Eleanor's death may have been an important contributory factor in the changing nature of his regime after 1290.

and because he had destroyed by burning – towns and churches and monasteries, – he is taken down from the gallows, and his belly opened, – the heart and bowels burnt to ashes, – and his head cut off for such faults, – because he had by these . . ., – maintained war, given protections, – seized lordship into his subjection – of the realm of another by his intrusions – His body was cut into four parts, – each hung by itself in memory of his name, – instead of his banner these are his standards – To finish his history, – at London is his head, – his body is divided in four good towns, – whereby to honour the isles – that are in Albania – And thus may you hear, – a lad to learn – to build in peace – It falls in his eye, – who hacks too high, – with the Wallace.

A similar punishment was meted out to Simon Fraser a year later, and is described in the *Song on the Execution of Sir Simon Fraser*:

To be a warning to all the gentlemen who are in Scotland . . . the head [Wallace's] to London Bridge was sent – to prison there, – Afterwards Simon Fraser, who was traitor and fickle, – Sir Edward our king, who is full of piety – sent the Wallace's quarters to his own country, to hand in four parts (of the country) to be their mirror, thereupon to think, in order that many might see – and dread – Why would they not take warning – of the battle of Dunbar – how ill they sped

Found on the Elderslie Wallace Monument, this is a copy of the plaque on the wall of St Bartholomew's Hospital, London, close to the spot where he was executed (see following page).

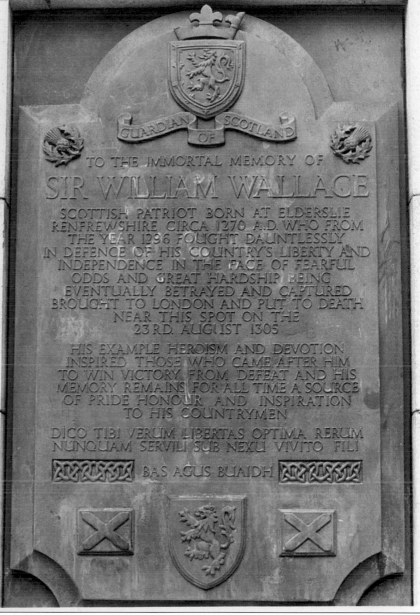

The monument commemorating the death of Edward I in July 1307 at Burgh-on-Sands. Earlier in the year the English King had recognised that his policy for settling Scotland may have been 'harsh and rigorous'. This was Edward I's way of explaining the continuing levels of resistance that he was still experiencing after 1305 when he established a new government for Scotland. He was campaigning against the new opposition movement led by Robert Bruce at the time of his death.

St Bartholomew's plaque, St Bartholomew's Hospital, near Smithfield, London. This panel commemorates William Wallace as 'Scottish patriot . . . put to death near this spot'.

The English had firmly established William Wallace's as the symbol of Scottish resistance by focusing attention on his capture, ritual trial and savage punishment in 1304 and 1305. There is no evidence that Wallace's death caused Robert Bruce to come out in open rebellion in 1306. Bruce was already developing his own plans in 1304, with or without Wallace's assistance. Undoubtedly, Wallace's savage execution on 23 August 1305 raised the political temperature in Scotland and perhaps expedited Bruce's own plans for revolt. Bruce and Wallace, however, represented two very different sides of the Scottish 'patriot' coin. Nationalist histories of the fourteenth and fifteenth centuries have placed them closer together than they were at the time. Yet Bruce, by going it alone in 1306, and gaining some military success in 1307, soon found himself on a similar journey to the one that Wallace embarked on in 1297. It was not, however, until 1307–8 that Bruce gained the same degree of popular support enjoyed by Wallace between 1297 and 1298.

It is clear that Robert Bruce was not the natural successor of William Wallace. Wallace and Robert Bruce deserve entirely separate reputations as Scottish 'patriot' heroes. The number of Wallace placenames, statues and memorials found in Scotland attest to the popular appeal of William Wallace. While, however, Blind Harry and *Braveheart* have undoubtedly exaggerated Wallace's efforts and somewhat distorted his reputation, there is no denying the real historical achievement of William Wallace. The Scottish political elite of Comyn, Balliol, Stewart and Bruce (albeit on it's fringe) wrote and spoke the language of nationalism and Scottish independence but no one acted on those words more passionately and with such utter lack of compromise than William Wallace between 1297 and 1305.

APPENDIX
ACCESS TO SITES

HISTORIC SCOTLAND

The sites listed below are manned and therefore subject to entry fees. All have the following standard opening times unless otherwise stated:

SUMMER: April–September, daily 9.30 a.m.–6.30 p.m.
WINTER: October–March, Monday–Saturday 9.30 a.m.–4.30 p.m., Sunday 2–4.30 p.m.

Caerlaverock Castle
Dirleton Castle
Linlithgow Palace
Melrose Abbey

WINTER: closed Thursday p.m. and all day Friday

Bothwell Castle
Dumbarton Castle
Dunfermline Abbey
Sweetheart Abbey

WINTER: daily to 5 p.m. (not 4.30 p.m.)

Stirling Castle

WINTER: closed

Balvenie Castle

All other sites are unmanned and open at any reasonable time.

ENGLISH HERITAGE SITES

SUMMER: April–September, daily 10 a.m.–6 p.m.
WINTER: November–March, daily 10 a.m.–4 p.m.

Carlisle Castle
Clifford's Tower, York
Lanercost Priory
Norham Castle

SUMMER: regularly

Alnwick Castle
Bamburgh Castle

OCCASIONAL OPENING

Bywell Castle

BIBLIOGRAPHY

PRIMARY SOURCES
(in translation except where stated)

Carmichael, F., Hamilton, F. and Shead, N. (eds). *History: Sources for the Study of the Scottish Wars of Independence 1249–1329*, Dundee, Scottish Consultative Council in the Curriculum, 1998

Coss, P. (ed.). *Thomas Wright's Political Songs of England*, Cambridge University Press, 1996

King, E. (ed.). *William Hamilton of Gilbertfield's Blind Harry's Wallace*, Edinburgh, Luath Press, 1998

Maxwell, H. (tr.). *Chronicle of Lanercost 1272–1346*, Glasgow, James Maclehose and Sons, 1907

—— (tr.). *Scalacronica by Sir Thomas Gray*, Glasgow, James Maclehose and Sons, 1907

Rothwell, H. (ed.). *The Chronicle of Walter of Guisborough* (Camden Third Series), London, Royal Historical Society, 1957

Skene, W.F. (ed.). *John of Fordun's Chronicle of the Scottish Nation*, The Historians of Scotland, Vol. IV, Edinburgh, 1872

Stevenson, J. (ed.). *Documents Illustrative of Sir William Wallace*, Edinburgh, Maitland Club, 1841 (*not translated*)

—— (ed.). *Documents Illustrative of the History of Scotland, 1286–1306* (2 vols), Maitland Club, Edinburgh, 1870 (*translates French texts only*)

Stones, E.L.G. (ed.). *Anglo-Scottish Relations 1174–1328: Some Selected Documents*, Oxford, Clarendon Press, 1963

Watt, D.E.R. (gen. ed.). *Scotichronicon by Walter Bower*, Vol. VI, Aberdeen, University Press, 1991

SECONDARY SOURCES

Barron, E.M. *The Scottish War of Independence*, Inverness, R. Carruthers & Sons, 1934

Barrow, G.W.S. *Scotland and its Neighbours in the Middle Ages*, London, Hambledon Press, 1992

——. *Robert Bruce*, Edinburgh University Press, 1988

——. *The Anglo-Norman Era in Scottish History*, Oxford, Clarendon Press, 1980

——. *The Kingdom of the Scots: Government, Church and Society from the Eleventh to the Fourteenth Century*, London, Edward Arnold, 1973

Broun, D., Finlay, R.J. and Lynch, M. (eds). *Image and Identity: the Making and Re-Making of Scotland through the Ages*, Edinburgh, John Donald, 1998

Close-Brook, J. *Exploring Scotland's Heritage: the Highlands*, Edinburgh, RCAHMS, 1980

Duncan, A.A.M. *Scotland, the Making of the Kingdom*, Edinburgh University Press, 1975

Fisher, A. *William Wallace*, Edinburgh, John Donald, 1986

Goldstein, R. James. *The Matter of Scotland, Historical Narrative in Medieval Scotland*, Lincoln, Nebraska, University of Nebraska Press, 1993

Grant, A. and Stringer, K.J. (eds). *Medieval Scotland: Crown, Lordship and Community, Essays Presented to G.W.S. Barrow*, Edinburgh University Press, 1993, repr. 1998

—— (eds). *Uniting the Kingdom: the Making of British History*, London and New York, Routledge, 1995

Jackson, R. and Wood, S. (eds). 'Images of Scotland', *The Journal of Scottish Education*, Occasional Paper Number One, Northern College, Dundee, 1997 – see especially Edward J. Cowan, 'The Wallace Factor in Scottish History', pp. 5–18

Keen, M. *The Outlaws of Medieval Legend*, London, Routledge and Kegan Paul, 1961

Kightly, C. *Folk Heroes of Britain*, London, Thames & Hudson, 1982 – see especially Ch. 6 'The Outlaw General'

Lynch, M. *Scotland, A New History*, London, Pimlico, 1991

McNeil, P.G.B. and Macqueen, H.C. *Atlas of Scottish History to 1707*, The Scottish Medievalists and Department of Geography, University of Edinburgh, 1996

Morton, G. *William Wallace: Man and Myth*, Stroud, Sutton Publishing, 2001

Prestwich, M. *Edward I*, New Haven and London, Yale University Press, 1998

——. *York Civic Ordinances 1301*, Borthwick Papers 49, University of York, 1976

Reid, N. (ed.). *Scotland in the Reign of Alexander III 1249–1286*, Edinburgh, John Donald, 1990

Ritchie, G. and Harman, M. *Exploring Scotland's Heritage: Argyll and the Western Isles*, Edinburgh, RCAHMS, 1985

Ross, D. *On the Trail of William Wallace*, Edinburgh, Luath Press, 1999

Shepherd, I.A.G. *Exploring Scotland's Heritage: Grampian*, Edinburgh, RCAHMS, 1986

Stell, G. *Exploring Scotland's Heritage: Dumfries and Galloway*, Edinburgh, RCAHMS, 1986

Stevenson, J.B. *Exploring Scotland's Heritage: the Clyde Estuary and Central Region*, Edinburgh, RCAHMS, 1985

Stringer, K.J. *Essays on the Nobility of Medieval Scotland*, Edinburgh, John Donald, 1985

Tabraham, C. *Scotland's Castles*, London, Batsford/Historic Scotland, 1997

Watson, F.J. *Under the Hammer: Edward I and Scotland 1286–1307*, East Linton, Tuckwell Press, 1998

Webster, B. *Medieval Scotland: the Making of an Identity*, London, MacMillan, 1997

Young, A. *Robert the Bruce's Rivals: the Comyns 1212–1314*, East Linton, Tuckwell Press, 1997, repr. 1998

——. 'Noble Families and Political Factions in the Reign of Alexander III', in N. Reid (ed.), *Scotland in the Reign of Alexander III 1249–86*

Young, A. and Stead, M.J. *In the Footsteps of Robert Bruce*, Stroud, Sutton Publishing, 1999

INDEX

References to illustrations are in italics.